Oh, shift!
Copyright © 2009 Jennifer Powers
Trademark pending.
www.ohshift.net

Back cover photo by Brian McDonnell – *bmacstudio.com*
Copy editing by Heather Strang – *heatherstrang.com*

Published by:
Blooming Twig Books LLC
PO Box 4668 #66675
New York, NY 10163-4668
www.bloomingtwigbooks.com

ISBN 978-1-933918-48-8

"oh, shi*f*t!"

JENNIFER POWERS

BLOOMING TWIG BOOKS / NEW YORK, NY

For Luis

.

.

.

the
most
beautiful
man
in
the
whole
wide
world

FAIR WARNING!

This book is about you. For you. But it can't stand alone. It needs YOU. The ever-evolving, beautiful individual that you are. You. The powerful, all-knowing fighter, seeker of light and joy.
Yes. All-knowing.

You have the answers.

This book is just a floodlight to help you see what is already inside of you. The path to the life you desire is there, waiting to be uncovered. My intention is to help you find it.

This book may be unlike any book you've ever read in that it treats you, the reader, not as a *receiver* of information but a *participant* in an experience.

It is meant to elicit reaction.
To spark thought.
Instigate change.
Promote movement.

This book expects as much from you as you expect from it.
Ponder its contents.
Debate it.
Consider the effects it can have on your life.
Apply it.
Talk about it.
Meditate on it.

Don't just read this book. Inhale it into you and
hold onto what serves you - exhale what doesn't.
Come back to it again and again.
Don't let it offend you.
Let it expand you.
You deserve to expand.
You deserve to thrive.
You deserve to define your life on your own terms.
You deserve to live every moment of every day
from a place of joy.
You deserve it all.
You can have it all.
And on your way to getting it,
never, ever forget how
f'in amazing you are.

Jennifer Powers
jennifer@jenniferpowers.com

TABLE OF CONTENTS

Oh, shift!

Just say it.

I'm a self-reflection whore.

I reflect to grow.
It's what I do.
I don't have it all figured out but what I do, I want to share.

Here's my promise to you.

This book can change your life.
But not in one hour, one day or even one read.
It will show you how to take baby steps towards *shifts*
that will collectively make a huge difference.

It will turn your mountains into molehills.
It will shed light on some of life's truths.
It will invite you to look at things differently.
It will get you *shift-faced*.

I promise.

One little letter

Year... 1989
Place... Granada, Spain
Lesson... Bueno

I was in my second year of college when I had the opportunity to study abroad in Spain.

My host family was nice. Rich too.

Mama Encarnita was sweeter than sugar and as wide as she was
tall. An amazing cook and a lover of red wine, she became my
instant BFF.

Jose, the host dad, didn't say much, but when he did he was
questioning the "politico Americano" which I knew (or cared)
little about. So we were happy to simply say hello in passing at
six in the morning when he was waking up for work and I was
stumbling in from the never-ending party scene on the streets
of Granada.

They had a daughter my age named Rosario, who loved to
poke fun at my big Jersey hair and my horrible Spanish accent.
Fun stuff.

I wasn't there two weeks when it happened.

The moment that will go down in history.

The story that Encarnita's family will tell every friend, neighbor and exchange student for as long as they walk the earth.

Mama Encarnita thought it would be fun to invite some extended family members to come meet me, so she planned a special dinner. Oh, and it *was* special.

There we were, sixteen of us. Cousins, in-laws, brothers and sisters, Rosario's English teacher Susanna, and Pedro, the tobacco shop owner from across the street.

Dinner was served. The Tempranillo was flowing and the mood got light. Mama Encarnita and her sister Anna made the most delicious dish I had ever put in my mouth. Chicken stewed in a rich tomato sauce together with eggplant and capers and a strong dose of fresh garlic. One word: *Yum-o-rama*.

Self conscious of my weight growing up, I was always hesitant to ask for seconds, especially around strangers. But I figured, when in Spain...EAT.

Soooo, in my best Spanish I asked for more chicken...

"Quiero mas polla, por favor."

Silence.

For three seconds.

Then an eruption of laughter so loud they could hear it in New Jersey. Wine and food went flying through noses clear across the table.

The women lost it. Pedro did a sign of the cross and got up to leave the room. Jose had a creepy grin on his face and his sixty-year-old brother Felipe looked aroused.

"What?"

I was definitely on the *outside* of an *inside*.

Rosario's English teacher finally leaned over and let me in.

"Chicken is *pollO* not *pollA*!" she said through a busted gut.

I wasn't surprised. I was, and still am, notorious for making that mistake. Masculine and feminine words just never made sense to me.

"So what? Is it really that funny?"

"Yes, you just said, 'I want more penis, please!'"

Oh what a difference
one little letter can make.

"Oh, shi*f*t!"

It's really quite simple.

Change the word that brings you down
to a word that lifts you up.

The difference is one little letter.

And it's a good one...*f*

Go ahead. Slip it in there right
between the "i" and the "t" and
then say it out loud.

Now, believe it or not, for some people that's a challenge.

Babs, one of my fellow New Jersey cronies, admitted that it took her great levels of concentration and effort to say the word *with* the f.

Mmmmm. You can take the girl out of Jersey...

But most people aren't like Babs.

Changing a word is easy. We actually do this all day long.

When talking to children, old people and CEOs, we tend to choose the more intelligent-sounding alternatives over our lazy *slanguage*.

"Yeah" becomes *"Yes."*

"You bet" becomes *"Certainly."*

"Dunno" becomes *"I'm not quite sure."*

Or we censor our more colorful language and opt for the G-rated version. (Think: *heck, fudge, darn, freakin', rear-end.*)

'Nuff said.

Why do we do that?

The words we choose help us

be what we want to be.

We do it for our children to **be** good role models.
We do it for our parents to **be** good children.
We do it in interviews to **be** a good candidate.
We do it at dinner parties to **be** a good guest.
We do it on first dates to **be** a good prospect.
We do it in the bedroom to **be** a good lover.

Why stop there?

In the moments of solitude, when no one
is around, you can choose your words so they

create a good impression on your life.

Words give you
power and **control**.

You are given a
blank canvas each day.

Your words are
your paint.

You are if you say you are.
You will if you say you will.

Tell yourself *you suck at golf* and you will.
Tell yourself *you'll never find a mate*. Done.
Tell yourself *you are always late* and you will be.
Tell yourself *you're fat*. You got it.
Tell yourself *you'll bomb the interview*. OK. No problem.

You call it.
It's your choice.
It's your life.

In a letter from a client:

Jennifer, I'm writing to tell you about a very powerful insight I had this past week.

*It happened one morning when my alarm went off. I hit snooze and then immediately went into self-talk, telling myself I was a **loser** for hitting my snooze button.*

When SUDDENLY a voice in my head (which sounded a bit like yours) said,

"Glenda, let's rephrase those words, shall we?"

*So, I thought about it for a moment and said to myself, "Oh, how **lucky** I am that I can take these extra nine minutes of rest, and how even more wonderful that I get to wake up to a brand new day, refreshed and ready!"*

Jennifer, I get it now. I am doing so much better at catching negative language and switching it around!

Isn't that the best?

Glenda M., 50

No, Glenda. YOU are the best.

Life is made up of a gazillion choices.

You make **hundreds** every day,

dozens every hour.

Think about it...

Food shopping
Channel surfing
Getting dressed
Making dinner
Answering the phone
Working late
Going out
Staying in

Based on the choices you make,
your day will play out one way or another.

Based on how your day goes,
your collective week will be determined.

Based on what kind of week you have,
your month will follow suit.

That flows into years and, of course, life.
You get the picture.

But here's what you may not get...

What you say will influence what you think.

What you think will influence how you feel.

How you feel will influence what you do.

What you do will influence your results.

...Every time.

This is a true domino effect.

Let's say you're told that you'll be given extra work and responsibility at your job but your salary will *not* be increased to reflect the changes.

You choose to **say**...
"Oh, sh*t!"

Which makes you **think**...
I'm being taken advantage of.

Which makes you **feel**...
Victimized, unappreciated, underpaid and miserable.

Which makes you **do**...
Show up at work with a scowl on your face, no initiative and a chip on your shoulder the size of Gibraltar.

Which **results** in...
You in your boss' office getting an attitude adjustment / written up / fired.

Dominoooooooooooooo.

Now imagine the same scenario but instead:

You choose to **say**...
"Oh, shift!"

Which makes you **think**...
I am being asked to take on more responsibilities because they value my work and qualifications.

Which makes you **feel**...
Flattered. Happy. Motivated.

Which makes you **do**...
Show up at work with a smile on your face, more initiative and a dozen donuts.

Which **results** in...
Your boss giving you a proverbial pat on the back / raise / promotion.

Groovy, huh?

Saying "Oh, sh*t!" is useless.

It does nothing for you.
It's a curse.
A purposeless expletive
that leaves you hanging
with no recourse.

Saying "Oh, shift!" is a choice.

It's not mandatory.
It's an option you have
every time something
happens in your life.

When you say "Oh, shi*f*t!" you redesign your thoughts, feelings and actions, which will ultimately redesign your life.

Now that's some cool shift.

Karma loogies in my food

Year... 2006
Place... Salem, Oregon
Lesson... Control

I wanted to open a new account at a bank that offered great terms. It was really close to my home and offered a $50 incentive to new clients. (Free money is good.)

I showed up and signed in at the lobby before taking a seat to wait for the next available banker. I looked over and saw that out of the three bankers, two were with clients and one, named David, was on the phone.

I was next in line so I figured as soon as he finished his call he would assist me.

B ored, I started to listen to his conversation. I then real- ized he was talking to some guy who was interested in buying his 1992 Honda Civic, which apparently was in great shape except for a small crack in the windshield and two dings on the passenger side door. The oil had been changed regu- larly, and he had all the records to prove it. It was recalled back in '93 for a wiring problem, and he hasn't had any trouble since...And on he went.

For twenty minutes.

I was getting seriously red in the neck. Steam was pouring out of my ears. My Jersey attitude was starting to creep to the surface as I thought to myself, "WHAT AM I, CHOPPED LIVER?"

David *finally* hung up the phone and moseyed over to see "what he could do for me." I asked him if he was on a lunch break. I mean, come on, he had to have been on his lunch break. There's no way he would have gone on like that about his car with me sitting within earshot waiting for him to call my frickin' name. Right?

When he told me his lunch break wasn't for another hour I lost it. My hands were shaking, and through a cottony-dry mouth I managed to tell him exactly what I felt about his customer service skills – and I didn't candy coat it.

I told him it was inexcusable to spend twenty minutes on a personal call when there was someone waiting in the lobby. And if he was going to treat new customers like this then he might wind up without a job, and in these trying times he should really kiss his customers AND his boss for giving him the privilege of being employed.

The kid just stood there with his hands in his pocket.

He didn't care.

Which got me even more pissed off.

So, I told him I needed to speak with his manager.

I told her what happened. She said she was sorry and that she would be sure to take care of the situation.

To avoid rewarding negative behavior, I told her that I couldn't in good conscious open up an account after such an experience.

And I left.

Without my account. Without my fifty bucks.

That stung.

But the real kick in the butt came a month later when my husband and I went out to dinner at the local Chili's. Our waiter, the food handler, controller of all quality and cleanliness as it pertains to our meal between the time it leaves the kitchen and the moment it's placed in front of us, approached our table and introduced himself as the one, the only, David.

I think some people call this Karma.

Call it what you want. It's there and it will find its way to you, because every choice you make will eventually affect your life.

The day you realize the impact your words, thoughts, feelings and actions have on your reality, you will have more control over your life…and fewer loogies in your food.

You so deserve that.

When you say "Oh, shift!" you will think and feel totally different...

Open-minded, like an optimistic problem-solving
super hero who's ready for anything.
When you feel that way, you will be unstoppable.
Your actions that follow will be purposeful, driven and
so damn amazing.

Choosing to say "Oh, shift!" gives you an open door.

Options.
A mindset that is intentional.

How?

"Oh, shift!" isn't just an exclamation, it's **a directive.**
The expression TELLS YOU TO DO SOMETHING.

It orders you to shift your perspective so you can react in a way
that supports **YOU IN GETTING WHAT YOU WANT.**

Genius.

Get creative.

Write **"Oh, shift!"** on a small piece of paper,
on the back of your hand, on the visor of your car.
Pin it to your wall or your refrigerator door...

Whisper it to yourself.

Shout it out loud.

Tattoo it on your butt for all I care.

Just be sure to keep this phrase front and center all the time.
You never know when you might need it.

CHOOSE
"Oh, shift!"

OVER
"Oh, sh*t!"

...and watch what happens.

The more
you do
the
better
your
life
will become.

What's all this shift about?

It's about choice.

Shifting lets you design your life

by choosing how you react

to everything that happens in it.

Sparks

Year... 1987
Place... New Jersey
Lesson... Missed opportunity

I remember getting into my very first fender bender. I was driving my souped-up '79 Camaro that had just been painted a perfect shiny maroon. The white pin stripe down the side matched the wide white wall tires. It was a hot car, and I felt even hotter behind the wheel.

On my way back from the paint and body shop, I stopped on a dime at a red light, but the big 'ol Caddy behind me didn't have the same luck.

T he lady driving the Cadillac slammed into my Camaro with such force she pushed me into the car in front of me. My brand new paint job was more than smudged – at both ends.

It got ugly pretty fast. The only thing bigger than my hair back then was my temper. I was PISSED OFF and I didn't have any qualms about showing it.

I got out of the car screaming at the Cadillac lady who, in my mind, was clearly responsible for this mess.

I laid into her. Ripped her a new one. She screamed right back at me, and our verbal catfight began.

W ell, the Cadillac lady got so mad at me for tearing into her, that when we exchanged contact information she used it to make a phone call to my parents. She told them how awful I was in the way I reacted to the accident.

Needless to say, I was grounded.

Being grounded made me miss going to the senior dance with my yummy crush Jeff Johnson.

O h, I was mad. But technically, I could only be mad at myself. It was *my* reaction to what happened that kept me from going to one of the most important events of my senior year. An event everyone insisted on talking about until graduation.

I could not control what happened (the accident), and that in and of itself would not have gotten me grounded. I could only control how I reacted to the accident, and *that* is what kept me from dancing cheek to cheek with Jeff.

In hindsight, I realized my reaction to that single event could have changed the course of my life. Who knows what sparks could have flown that night between me and Jeff?

If I had kept my mouth shut and handled the car accident with a bit of grace, maybe Jeff and I could have had a beautiful wedding, a honeymoon in Hawaii, and by now be divorced with two kids, fighting over our vacation home in the Hamptons.

You get the point.

It's the little choices that collectively
make up the big picture —

LIFE.

Change your choices,
change your life.

The Tyrant Boss

Year... 2000
Place... Houston, Texas
Lesson... Choice

I used to work for a tyrant. A small business owner who annoyed the shi*ft* out of me every day. Her demands were completely unreasonable. Short deadlines, overtime without pay, working on weekends without so much as a "thank you" in return.

And her bossy, grumpy demeanor totally made me sick to my stomach. Whenever I pulled into the parking garage and saw her car there, I cringed.

She pushed all my buttons.

No.

Correction: I *let* her push my buttons.

T he money was good, the benefits supreme, and there was a lot of room for growth; so I stayed in that job for two years, living a miserable nine-to-five existence.

Every day I left the office frustrated, angry and feeling powerless.

And I *was* powerless.

I was powerless because I was reacting to my tyrant boss in a way that was destructive to me. In other words, I was letting her get the best of me, and no one deserves that.

I suffered. My husband suffered. My self-esteem suffered – even my dog suffered. All because I failed to realize that I had a choice.

A ctually, I had two choices. I could have quit or I could have shifted by choosing my feelings instead of letting her choose them for me.

When something happens that makes you feel crappy, who's responsible for you feeling that way?

Did you know that when you let someone or something determine your emotions, you are serving up your power to them on a platter? Giving it away.

It's not their fault. They don't *take* your power.

You *give* it to them.

I gave that tyrant the power to rule my emotional state even when I wasn't on the clock. She haunted my every waking hour, and it sucked.

H er fault? No. All mine.

But I loved blaming her. At the time I didn't understand that no one has the power to make me feel *this* mad, frustrated or underappreciated…unless I let them. And boy, did I let her.

I can't get those two years back, but I'm not one to miss out on a lesson. So, here it is:

You emotional state is decided by you.
And your reality is determined by the way
you choose to react to the situations or people
that show up in your life.

What people say or do is what they say or do. That's it. You can't control them, and frankly, you wouldn't want to. But you *can* control how you react to them.

We often forget this.

M any of us are happy to take the victim role, whining that this person or that circumstance ruined our day, our week, or our life.

I call "Bull-Shift!"

No one or no thing is responsible for any part of your reality. Only you.

The way you react to the things that happen in your life will determine how you *experience* life.

And as I mentioned before – Karma always has a way of showing up. Always.

I found out several years after leaving the job that the tyrant lost two of her biggest accounts and had to file bankruptcy. Oh, and her husband ran off with the secretary.

Ouch.

How much time do you spend

before deciding how to respond to the people and events
that show up *(or throw up)* in your life?

Inquiring minds want to know.

Shifting is like learning how to play golf. (But not as boring.)

How did Tiger Woods get so good?

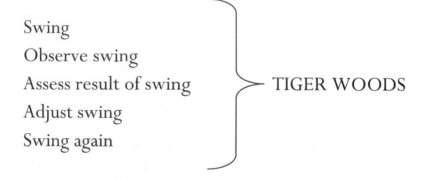

Swing
Observe swing
Assess result of swing
Adjust swing
Swing again

} TIGER WOODS

Not complicated. Just good old hard work.

Practice your Shi*f*t.

(This is fun.)

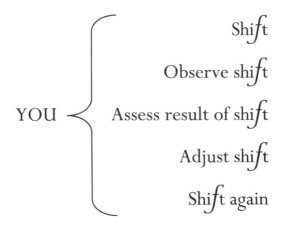

YOU {
Shi*f*t

Observe shi*f*t

Assess result of shi*f*t

Adjust shi*f*t

Shi*f*t again

After each shi*f*t ask yourself what worked and what didn't,
then adjust as needed and proceed accordingly.*
You *and* your life will get better each time.

*If you skip the observe, assess and adjust part, you will never get better —
you'll get frustrated. Trust me on this one.*

Shifting builds confidence in who you are and what's possible for you.

Make 1 small shift and you'll be more confident to make another.

Make 3 small shifts and you'll develop a pattern.

Make 20 small shifts and you will feel like a pro.

Then you'll be on your way to taking a BIG shift.

And who doesn't like that?

Be a shift head

You can do this.

It took me a long time to admit that I had to change something about myself if I expected anything in my life to change. After all, who else is going to rescue me? I had a lot to learn, and I still do. But now I feel like I have so much more control over what I experience because I choose how I am going to feel or react to the stuff that goes on around me.

Carolyn R., *39*

Carolyn soooo gets it.

Carolyn is a *shift head.*

Wanna be like Carolyn?

The 7 STEPS

to becoming a shi*f*t head.

Step # 1 : *Get in the game*

H ave you ever played dodgeball?

God I hated that game. I was always the first to get hit.

One day in the 7ᵗʰ grade I got beamed really hard in my ass and everyone laughed. I don't know which stung worse, my ball-burned butt, or my bruised ego. I cried like a baby, right there in front of everyone.

See, getting hit on any other part of my body would have been fine, but in grade school I had a funny – (read: large) shaped butt that kids loved to laugh at.

The thing about dodgeball is that you're supposed to *avoid* getting hit. But eventually you will. Everyone gets hit at some point.

It's kinda like life.

You get pummeled by negative situations and people all day long, and you don't get to choose where or when they hit you.

Sometimes, you will get hit where you are most vulnerable.

And it will hurt.

But it's not getting hit that you are meant to worry about. More importantly, it's how you react when you *do* get hit.

Being a shi*f*t head means you are

on the lookout for the big red rubber balls

being wailed at you from every direction.

You see them coming and you know how to duck, jump, dive and hop at just the right moment to get out of their way before they slam you in the ass... and keep you in therapy for six years. But, I digress...

Getting hit is part of the game, and not always within your control. But how you react when you get hit is always within your control.

As a shi*f*t head, *now* when I play dodgeball and get hit, I have a totally different reaction.

I thank God I can sit down and stop playing that stupid game.

Step#2 : *Be a quitter*

Shi*f*t heads quit blaming everything and
everyone for their life being the way it is.
They realize that although it's easier to fault others,
it's clearly not the most powerful way to live.
So they QUIT.

Shi*f*t heads quit having pity parties for themselves.
Waste of time. Life's short.
So they QUIT.

Shi*f*t heads quit doing what they've always done.
Because they know if they don't, they'll always get
what they've always gotten.
So they QUIT.

Step #3 : *Be insistent and consistent*

To create a shi*f*t that is sustainable, you have to work at choosing your reactions wisely every single day.

Go into this process knowing that trying harder will not necessarily make shi*f*t stick. Trying hard will create shi*f*t in your life, but it's the insistent and consistent effort that will keep it around.

The journey to becoming a shi*f*t head has a beginning and end, but not only one. Each day when you wake up, you begin the process all over again. You get to decide how you will react to everything your day presents to you.

Oh, and you'll slip and backslide for sure.

It's part of the process.

Again, you have the power to choose whether or not you'll get up and keep going.

Did you know you had this much power?

Saaa-weeeeeeeeet!

Step#4: *Stay in the moment*

B
eing a shift head means standing in your power to choose your reality, right here right now. Not tomorrow, not next year.

Right now. That's where you have to live if you plan on taking control of your life.

In the NOW.

To shift, you have to be present in the moment to choose your feelings, thoughts and reactions appropriately.

When something negative happens and you react based on what it will mean for your future, you have missed the opportunity to control your present. You have lost your power. You gave it away. Poof.

For example, when you miss your bus and you think about the downward spiral effect it will have on your day (the future), you miss the opportunity to react appropriately in the moment (the present).

When your teenage son gets an "F" in Algebra and your knee-JERK reaction is to fast forward with worry about how he will ever make it to college, your reactions will be lame-o at best.

By staying in the moment you keep the situation in perspective so you can choose your words, thoughts, feelings and actions more rationally. And therefore, more effectively.

Ta-daaa!

Focusing on the future negates the present.

Like Confucius said...

*"You must stay in the present
if you want to be powerful there."*

**Well, if he didn't say that,
he should have.**

Step #5 : *Raise your pain threshold*

Becoming a shift head requires you to change, and let's face it, change can be painful.

Many of us stay in a less than ideal situation because we fear the pain associated with change.

It's like that extra body weight you're carrying around. You feel the pain it causes you every time you go into the closet to get dressed. But if you haven't done anything about it, then my guess is the pain of restricting calories and exercising five days a week trumps even the awful discomfort of a too-tight waistline.

Becoming a shift head will be uncomfortable. It will stretch you. And that's good.

Because when you stretch you grow.

Yes, it may be difficult. Change often is. But like anything, the more you shift the easier it will become.

It's a lot like trying to write with your opposite hand. At first attempt you will feel awkward and incompetent. Your tendency will be to put the pen in the other hand where it is comfortable.

But if you resist that temptation and you keep writing, even though it is uncomfortable, you will eventually begin to improve. You will train yourself to write with a different hand.

You can so *handle* this.

Step#6: *Be a rebel*

S hift heads march to the beat of a different drum. And their friends and loved ones may not *feel the beat*, if ya' know what I mean.

Choosing to react in ways others are not used to may ruffle some feathers. If they can't handle the change, it may require you to break free from the flock you fly with.

Think of that friend, co-worker or family member you can always count on to bitch with about anything. He or she may not be thrilled to find out that you no longer aspire to trash the world.

This is tough. But you, my fellow shift head, are tougher.

Like Mom always said, "Tell me who your friends are, and I'll tell you who you are."

Birds of a feather flock together.

You're a flamingo now. They choose to remain pigeons.

Fly away little birdie.

Fly away.

Step#7 : *Be a victor, not a victim*

My friend Tina, who has been blind from birth, taught me this. She knows the difference and she chooses to be a victor in her life, and mine, every day.

I'm not sure Tina was ever anything but a shi*f*t head. It's like she was born into the role.

Most of us aren't like Tina. You have to choose to be *reborn* into the role of a **victorious** shi*f*t head.

And in doing so you choose to see yourself not as a victim of circumstance but a **conqueror** of all challenges.

You'll never find Tina blaming her reality on the fact that she drew the short straw. Nope. Tina sees every straw as **purposeful** and **positive**.

Tina looks at everything that happens – good or bad – in a way that serves her, not defeats her.

Sometimes I think Tina has
better sight than most of us.

Shift or get off the pot

Are you ready?

I f you bought this book I assume it's because there's some part of your life you want to change.

If someone gave you this book, that person loves you enough to hold up the mirror so you can see that your life could stand some changing. Go kiss them. There is no act more brave, noble or loving.

However this book found its way into your hands, it came to you in the form of a gift. Either by yourself or someone else, you have been gifted.

Gifted with the grand opportunity to experience freedom, choice, power, happiness, success, control, peace, joy, love, truth, health.

You name it.

Whatever you are longing for, the principles in this book will show you how to get it.

No shi*f*t. You can have it — if you are ready.

T ake this quickie *Readiness Assessment*. (No pen required)

Count on your fingers how many of these statements you agree with.

○ I am ready to stop blaming everything and everyone for my life being the way it is.

○ I am ready to stop feeling inadequate, powerless, unaccomplished, victimized, argumentative, lame, undervalued, unorganized, unsuccessful, unlucky, lost, lonely, sad, fat, ugly, sick and tired.

○ I am ready to be a different person.

○ I am ready to accept change into my life.

○ I am ready to feel deserving of all the benefits that come with changing the way I react to life.

How many fingers do you have up?
Five? You're ready.
Less than 5? Don't sweat it. I'll have you convinced you're ready by the end of this section.

Let's take a look at each of these statements to see what I can do to prepare you for the time of your life...

I am ready to stop blaming everything and everyone for my life being the way it is.

Have you ever said the following... ?

"I would be happy if my **husband** would just..."

"My job sucks because my **boss** is an ass."

"When my **kids** move out I will finally be able to..."

"I'm overweight because my **schedule** doesn't allow time for exercise."

"I am just not a **lucky** person."

"If the **economy** were better I wouldn't be in this financial mess."

"Damn **politicians**."

"My **friends** don't appreciate me enough."

"It's my **mother's** fault."

Etc.

If you have ever used lame-o excuses like these to
avoid holding yourself accountable for the
outcome of your life, you are normal.

But who wants to be normal?

Normal ≠ Good

Just because something is normal,
doesn't mean it's good. And
   you so deserve to be good.
      Better than good, actually.

          So, take a look at your life.
             All of it.

               What are you blaming others for?
                 When will you be ready to stop?

How does NOW grab you?

Own your
own shift.

Do yourself a favor.

Stop relying on everyone else to make you happy or feel appreciated.

There is no way you're going to win at this game called life by relying on your herd of scapegoats.

You deserve better than that. The only person you can point your blaming finger at is you. After all, this is *your* life. No one but *you* is responsible for your happiness and well-being.

You're the boss, applesauce.

Own it.

Next...

I am ready to stop feeling inadequate, powerless, unaccomplished, victimized, argumentative, lame, undervalued, unorganized, unsuccessful, unlucky, lost, lonely, sad, fat, ugly, sick and tired.

Careful. At first glance, this seems like a no-brainer. My focus groups of Potential Shift Heads (PSH) thought it was, and they all screamed, "OF COURSE I AM READY TO STOP FEELING THIS WAY!" I mean, think about it. Who wouldn't?

But it's not that simple.

In an interview, one PSH told me, *"I don't always remember I have the power to choose. I feel victimized and powerless."*

I loved his honesty, but I had to lay down the truth for him, and I'll do the same for you right now.

You feel these feelings because at some level or another they serve you.

Yes.

That's right.

You may not think it serves you to live in sub-par conditions, but it does. Not necessarily in a good way. But the truth is, we only keep things around (including feelings of inadequacy and powerlessness) if they serve us at some level.

I n the psychology world they call this "secondary gain."

For example, when I asked one of my clients how the **extra twenty pounds** she's been trying to take off for the **last twenty years** is serving her, she recognized it as one of those "secondary gains." (No pun intended.)

After some coaching, she realized that she is "willingly" keeping that extra weight on because it is one way she can feed her constant need to stay small so others can feel big. (Ironic pun intended.)

She told me she can use her overweight status to make other women feel more comfortable around her, which is something she has always struggled with because she is so attractive.

By keeping the weight on, she feels more approachable, less threatening, and therefore more liked.

Yikes!

S teven admitted that he has stayed an hourly employee at work because he doesn't want the heavy burden of making important decisions in a management role. He said he couldn't stand making a mistake in front of his peers. *Steven chooses to remain powerless, and it serves to protect him from embarrassment.*

B onnie said she never went to college because her grandfather, who raised her, always told her she wasn't smart enough. She loved him dearly. So much so that she didn't want to prove him wrong by actually going to college. *Her feeling of being unaccomplished serves to honor her grandfather.*

K alista admitted that if she were just a little bit more organized she could double the revenue of her accounting business. Diving deeper, we discovered that success scares the shift out of her, because if she were running a fully thriving business she wouldn't have time to spend with her kids. *Staying unorganized helps Kalista avoid the conditions she believes would make her less of a mother.*

QUESTION:

How does it serve you to feel inadequate, powerless, unaccomplished, victimized, argumentative, lame, undervalued, unorganized, unsuccessful, unlucky, lost, lonely, sad, fat, ugly, sick or tired?

When you answer this question and see how absolutely self-defeating it is to feel this way, then you are one step closer to being ready to shi*ft*.

You can't fix what you don't know is broken.

So go sit down with a cup of tea (or vodka) and do some serious soul searching around that question.

Self-awareness is your friend. The more you know about what makes you tick, the easier it is to fine tune your clock.

Moving on…

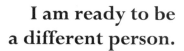

I am ready to be
a different person.

T his is a goodie.

In my earlier career as a weight loss counselor, I learned that one of the biggest struggles overweight people have with losing weight is being faced with a new identity.

Many people identify with carrying around extra weight. It's the mask they hide behind or the rock under which they shove deeply-seated issues.

Shedding that weight means identifying themselves as a completely different person AND being seen by others as a different person.

Same thing with becoming a shift head.

You will adopt a new identity. You will react to the world differently and therefore will have a different experience. You will change on the inside and those changes will be reflected in your actions on the outside.

You will be a different person. And you'll want to be ready.

You are ready to be a different person when you recognize that the way you are being is not getting you the results you want.

You are ready to be a different person when you give yourself permission to let go of who you are to make room for who you want to be.

You are ready to be a different person when you are willing to say "goodbye" to the old you and "hello" to what's possible.

**Letting go is hard,
but necessary to move forward.**

If you get stuck, think of it not as letting go of something old but as grabbing on to something new.

Cool.

I am ready to accept change into my life.

Many things will change when you become a shi*f*t head. When you decide you are ready to be a different person you can almost simultaneously expect to have a different life experience. You can't make a change like this and expect the other areas of your life to stay the same.

Greater levels of success, more opportunities, new friends, less pain, more joy, new hobbies and new language are just a few of the changes you can expect.

This means that those who loved being around you before might resent you now. And those who avoided you before might be magnetically attracted to you.

It also means that the conversations you have will change. Think of all that time you spend talking about how stupid others are or complaining about your job. What will you talk about now?

Your word choices will also change. Phrases like, *I'm lame, Life sucks, What a disaster, and You're a jerk* won't have a place in your vocabulary.

Expect your moods to change.

Are you ready to spend less time feeling down and more time smiling? Sounds like a silly question, but take a moment to answer it, because shi*f*ting really *will* turn that frown upside down. Guaranteed.

You can do this.
And make no apologies for it. Own it, just like you've owned the way you've been up until now.

Every choice you make dictates your life experience. And when you choose differently, change is inevitable.

And finally.

Drum roll please...

I am ready to feel deserving of all the benefits that come with changing the way I react to life.

When I asked my focus groups of PSH's to comment on their readiness as it pertains to **feeling deserving,**
I got this response:

(Silence.)

Deserving?
Me?

Now, *you* may be saying, "Heck yeah, I'm deserving!"
But do you really feel it?
Are you acting deserving?
I love you, so I am going to be honest with you.
You probably aren't.

To feel and act deserving you have to forget every-thing you were ever told that made you feel guilty.

Your parents and grandparents told you something equivalent to: *"I had to walk six miles uphill, both ways, through the snow to get to school each day."*

Guilt.

You were coaxed to clean your plate by being reminded of the starving kids in Africa.

Guilt.

And depending on what spiritual education you had, there was no room for deserving-ness in a world of sinners.

Guilt. Guilt. Guilt.

We were brainwashed to believe that much of what we have, we don't deserve.

Few of us were told the truth…

You deserve everything wonderful that you have *and* everything that is on its way to you.

You deserve it.

All of it.

The only thing you have to do is be open to receiving it.

It's *yours,* for crying out loud!

Don't apologize for it.

Don't negate it.

Don't feel guilty about it.

Accept it.

Embrace it.

Love it.

Feels good, doesn't it?

Here's more good news...

Life

does not

have to be

difficult,

painful,

negative

or a struggle.

You

have

a

choice.

S ure you will have your challenges, but know this:

Life is meant to flow.

Like a leaf floating down a river you roll with the current, the ups and downs, over and around obstacles – going with it, not fighting against it.

So many of us live more like a salmon than a leaf, swimming upstream, against the natural flow. Using all our strength to conquer the greater force that engulfs us.

Why do we do that?

When will we let go and realize that the stream is flowing in the direction it's meant to go, and we are meant to go with it?

Here is the trick.

Explore your own enculturation.

What or who led you to feel, react, think, choose, judge the way you do? It may not be pretty or even fun to dig that deep. But believe me, it's worth it.

L ook at what you are willing to let go of.

What beliefs don't serve you?

What "lessons" or "teachings" will you ditch to make room for new ones?

Do not ignore this step.

If you think you can, think again.

We have *all* been programmed with belief systems that keep us from living a joyful life.

Find yours and call them out.

Then replace them with beliefs, lessons, teachings, thoughts, choices, feelings and reactions that serve you.

Help with this can be found in a good counselor.

Don't be ashamed. Every rock star sees a counselor.

Life can be easy, joyful, painless and juicy delicious… if you let it.

It's all up to you, oh powerful one.

So, now I ask you...

Are you ready?

- *Will you stop blaming others for the things you don't like about your life?*
- *Are you ready to stop feeling powerless?*
- *Are you willing to let go of who you are to embrace who you can be?*
- *Are you prepared to accept the changes that will naturally come as a result of these shifts?*
- *Can you give yourself permission to feel deserving of the benefits these changes will bring you?*

If you answered a resounding YES to all of the above then you are ready to join the movement and shi*f*t like a mutha!

Let's do this.

Oh, and be kind with yourself on this journey.

Go easy.

Take your time.
(But not too much, it's slightly limited.)

Get a load of this shift

New concepts to wrap your shifty little head around.

You're not in control of everything

Time... Now
Place... Right here
Lesson... Control **this**

W e are all part of a system called nature. Nature is very unique in that it's one of the few things we don't have to control. Sure we intervene, but it doesn't need us to in order to function and sustain itself. That's because if left untouched, everything in nature is in perfect order.

All by itself.

Imagine that.

When things go awry, nature *shifts* to bring things back into harmony.

Our natural environment has exactly what it needs in every moment.

Enter the human,
stage left.

A s part of this system, we have evolved into thinking, rational beings. But that doesn't mean we are no longer a part of the system; it just makes us think we can *control* the system.

We can't.

We are a part of it and not immune to it.

We human types tend to forget that, though. We constantly take actions that go against the flow of nature in an effort to make our lives "better."

If we don't like the way any part of the system is developing and sustaining itself around us, we cut it down, poison it, hunt it, medicate it, extinguish it, attack it, declare war on it, label it dangerous, or simply curse its existence.

And it almost always bites us in the butt.

T hat's so human; going against the natural flow of the system. If we don't think something is good, fair, profitable or convenient, we do whatever it takes to change or control it.

But think about it. How many events happen on earth everyday that *don't* seem good, fair, profitable or convenient?

Ever watch the *Discovery* channel where the baby gazelle gets eaten by a lion? The unhatched penguin that freezes to death? What about the tsunamis, hurricanes and tornados that devastate towns and villages in minutes?

Dutch Elm Disease is one of the most destructive plant diseases of the 20th century. The fungus invades the vascular system of an elm and prohibits water movement in the tree. Without water the leaves and branches begin to wilt and eventually the elm dies.

The disease has killed millions of innocent trees and its origin remains an enigma.

This is nature.

It will take its course and leave little room for intervention, and often no explanation.

So how does all this apply to you?

Look at your life.

How many things happen to you that don't seem
good, fair, profitable or convenient?

Exactly, a lot.

How many of these things
can you *really* control?

The things that happen aren't happening
TO you, **FOR** you or **AGAINST** you.

They are just happening.

You are not here to control **what happens**.

Your job is to control **how you react** to what happens.

The way you react to everything that happens
will determine how your life unfolds
from that point on.

A simple illustration.

The stock market takes a dive.

Mark, Kelly and Jim all lose their shorts.

Mark panics, feels vulnerable and sells all his shares.

Kelly, experiencing the same loss, chooses to see this as an opportunity and buys more while the price is low.

Jim is a scaredy cat and is afraid to do anything, so he doesn't.

Eleven months later when the market shifts,
Kelly makes out the best,
Jim does okay,
and Mark is too busy kicking himself to do the math.

The reality was the same for all three people: the stock market took a tumble and they all lost money. There was nothing any of them could do to control or prevent that from happening.

But each of them had *control over how they reacted* to it. They each reacted in a different way, so they each got different results.

Easy.
Like pie.

OK.

One more time,

because it's important.

Things really don't happen TO you.

Things just happen.

It's how you react to those things

that gives you control

of your life.

The question is:

How do you control your reactions?

I'm so glad you asked.

A trip to the head

You are head driven.
You live in your head and you go there for approval,
rationale, decisions and, of course, your reactions.

In your head you decide how you will
react to everything that happens.

YOU have a choice.

But here's the rub.

Two people live in your head and they are both **YOU.**

Allow me to introduce **YOU**
to your Ego and your Self.

Your Ego is your dark side.

Because it is dark,

the Ego thrives and feeds on pain and struggle.

The fiend, bully, troll, brute. The devil, if you will.

It longs for struggle, challenge and upset.

Looks for it. Fights for it. Feeds off of it.

Actually, your Ego is happiest when it is miserable and in pain.

Funny little bugger.

Your Self is your light side.

Because it is light,

the Self naturally sees the bright side of things.

The angel, peacemaker, light seeker. The buddha, if you will.

It wants to be happy. It lives for joy and peace.

And, when it can get a word in edgewise, it fights for it.

T he Ego and the Self (as I call them) are the two parts of each of us. Forget what these words mean in their psychological context. Just picture the Ego on your left shoulder and the Self on the right, whispering into your opposing ears.

Every time something happens in your life, a power struggle between your Ego and your Self ensues.

In your head there is a mental boxing match between the two opposing parts of you.

Your Ego fights for a reaction that involves struggle, pain and emotional destruction; and your Self fights hard for a reaction that results in joy, peace and freedom.

Back and forth they go.

They each have a voice, and they each want to be heard.

The less obvious problem is that too many of us let our Ego win.

I n our culture the Ego has a louder voice, more influence and power. As a result, we have a tendency to default to a negative, painful reaction because that's the way our Ego likes it.

Case in point...

I accidentally cut someone off on the freeway the other day. Looking back in my rear view mirror, I can tell you that the finger gesture the guy flipped me was NOT a *thumbs up*.

His knee-JERK reaction came straight from his Ego. His Self was willing and able to react in a way that was less emotionally disruptive, but the guy let his Ego snuff it out. When I accidentally cut him off, he had a choice to make: React from Self or Ego?

He clearly chose Ego.

T hink about the last time something unpleasant happened.

What was your knee-JERK reaction?

It's ok. You can admit it.

I do.

When things don't go my way, my Ego tries to shout the loudest. And to be honest, it sometimes wins.

This happens to the best of us.

That's because we've got human blood running through our veins. And we humans are far from perfect.

But we *are* malleable.

Whew.

How did our Ego get such a loud voice?

I'll tell you how.

The same way we came to believe we were so undeserving.

Our enculturation.

The last several generations have lived through, heard about, and read endless stories of struggle, pain and misfortune. *(Think: famine, slavery, race and gender inequality, WWI, the Great Depression, WWII, Vietnam, AIDS, 9-11.)*

As a result of our experience and education, we were literally hardwired to believe that pain, struggle and hardship are the status quo.

Sure, we have been given many opportunities. But think about it, how many of those opportunities came without pain, struggle or hardship?

Don't our soldiers FIGHT and DIE for our freedom? Don't we often have to SACRIFICE one thing for another? Find me a pharmaceutical drug that doesn't have six pages of ADVERSE side effects.

N ot to mention....

Every day at 6pm & 10pm we allow ourselves to be subjected to the most sensationalistic view of local and world events via the nightly news, which only seems to report on PAIN, STRUGGLE, DEATH, CRIME, FEAR, DISEASE, WAR and STRIFE.

All of this programming has trained our Ego to believe it's in charge and able to control our every reaction. This tends to make our knee-JERK reaction to even minor events, flaws or setbacks **Ego-driven by default.**

For example, when I look in the mirror, my knee-JERK reaction is not my Self saying, "You are so good-looking." Instead, it's usually my Ego turning me around, making a disgusted face and saying something like, "Fat ass!"

You get my drift. I know you do.

H ave you ever met really nice, happy people and wondered how they got to be that way?

It's not that they don't have an Ego. They do. The difference is that they don't let it have as much influence, voice and strength. They snuff the Ego's voice out. Resist its temptation. Ignore its desires. Shut it down so they can let their Self's voice come through louder and clearer.

Like you, they have a choice.

They choose joy and peace over sadness and pain.

They choose positivity over negativity.

They choose light over dark.

They choose silver lining over gloomy clouds.

They choose.

Same goes for the Negative Nellie Naysayers. They have a choice and they choose to let their Ego control their reactions. In other words, they react in ways that cause them pain and emotional destruction.

They too have a Self, but they choose to ignore it *and* its wishes to react in a way that is peaceful and harmonious.

So that begs the question...

When something crappy happens in your life,
which one typically controls *your* reactions?

EGO
SELF

(Check one and be honest. No one is looking.)

The trick to being a shift head

is to give your Self more power than your Ego.

In order to undo years of programming, your Self has to be stronger, more tenacious, tireless, adamant, consistent, almost obsessive compulsive until the Ego backs down and shuts up.

It sounds more difficult than it is, but then again – you've got this whole book to show you the way.

Rock it out.

A conversation between two pieces of shi*f*t.

Dearest Ego,

You are so overpowering all the time. Why do you keep snuffing me out?

With joy,

Self

Yo Self:

If I let go of my incessant search for ways to suffer, then what the hell would I do all day? And anyway, why don't you just try and stop me, you big sissy.

With pain,

Ego

Dear Ego:

Here's the thing. For some reason I have let you overpower me and it seems like I am now numb to the effects. It feels like I have been asleep, like when I sit on my foot for too long and it gets all numb. But every once in a while, when I fight hard for happiness and win the power struggle, I start to feel alive and get that tingly feeling. And it feels good.

In that moment, if I am not careful you will sit on me again and put me back to sleep. That's why I have to keep moving. I will not continue to play small so you can feel big. I will keep fighting and you will no longer overpower me.

I will consciously and consistently look for ways to be stronger than you. And no matter how much you fight, or how loud you scream, I will scream louder because I deserve to be heard.

Your constant complaining and negative chatter will be missed at first, but after awhile I'll get used to hearing the sound of my own sweet voice saying, "Oh, shi*ft*!"

With joy,

Self

P.S. I still love you.

Q.

What if I try to shut my Ego up but I can't? Sometimes I am so angry I can't see straight!

A.

So you are angry, seeing red and feeling like you need a Valium to calm down. Don't do anything. Just observe yourself in that moment of fiery-red fury. Examine the presence of your Ego and its attempt to fuel your pain. Remember, it lives for pain and suffering and it's not ashamed to fight for it. Like a bulldog, it clamps its jaws into any opportunity it has to roll around in pure misery.

Be with that for a moment. Look at the Ego in all of its disgusting glory and recognize that it's only one part of you.

Not the whole you, but part of you.

Honor it. Observe it.

Be gentle and patient with yourself.

This is a process of self-discovery and an unfolding of a new you. Sometimes we try to skip this moment of simple examination. But you'll be so much more effective when you allow space for it. Your awareness will grow, and you will be an expert on the subject of YOU.

The more you know about anything, the better prepared you are to deal with it.

Why take a shift?

Cause it feels soooo good.

Every shift, no matter how big or how small,
will give you control over your feelings.

Every shift will contribute to your
physical health and well-being.

Every shift will greatly benefit
your social experience.

Every shift will affect the lives
of those around you.

Every shift will redefine
your experience on an
emotional,
physical,
social and
global
level.

Yes, global.

Emotionally

When you shift you take charge of your emotions and own them. You stop blaming other people and circumstances for your feelings.

You stand in your power
by holding yourself accountable for your own reality.

With every shift you are molding your emotions and exercising your power of choice. You choose your feelings instead of letting *them* choose *you* based on circumstances that are out of your control.

When you shift you
redefine the feelings
that will ultimately
redefine your reality.

Shi*f*ting means choosing your feelings.

No *thing*,
no *event*,
no *person*,
has the power
to make you feel:
inadequate, powerless,
unaccomplished, victimized,
argumentative, lame, undervalued,
unorganized, unsuccessful, unlucky,
lost, lonely, sad, fat, ugly, sick or tired.

Only you.
It's your choice.

This is YOUR SHI*f*T!

Got it?

Good.

Physically

When you shift you contribute to your physical well-being. You control the rate of your heart and the pressure of your blood pumping through your veins. You manage your breath and allow it to feed you oxygen, energy and health.

When you shift you redefine how your mind will affect your body.

It is a decision, and it's yours to make. In every moment you get to decide how you will *let* your body feel.

Will you let your mind go awry and have your body react accordingly, sucking the air right out of your lungs? Or will you manage those thoughts so that your body gets the steady flow of air it needs to maintain a healthy state?

It doesn't take a genius to know that constant fluctuations of heart rate, blood pressure and breathing do not make a healthy person.

M y good friend Dina works in a doctor's office and her mother loves to call her and talk about all the crap that's going on in her life and the world.

This drives Dina crazy.

I asked her to do some research to see what effect these annoying phone calls had on her physical health.

Dina took her resting blood pressure before and after receiving a call from her mother on three separate occasions.

The effects of the annoying phone calls on Dina's body?

BEFORE THE CALL:
Average Blood Pressure: 120/60

AFTER THE CALL:
Average Blood Pressure: 140/87

Now, I'm no MD, but come on.
With a mother like that, who needs terrorism?

Once Dina realized she had a choice, she was able to shift the way
she reacted to her mother. She decided she was no longer
going to be a victim of her mother's toxic effects.
As a result, her blood pressure is
a solid 120/60 before *and* after the call.

Shifting can help you manage your health by controlling the way
you react to life's little annoyances.

Socially

Apart from the inner workings of YOU, there is the external influence that shifting has on others.

When you shift, you redefine yourself on a social level.

How?

Your reactions to life and happenstance will cause others to define you in one way or another. That usually translates into: *"I like you, or I don't like you"* or *"I want to be around you, or I want to avoid you"* or *"I want to give you opportunities, or I don't want to."* And so on.

How you show up determines who (and what) you will attract into your experience.

You may already know this, but it's always worth hearing again. However, if this is new for you, you'll want to pay close attention, because this is the really important part. So important, in fact, that some people call it the *SECRET* to making all your dreams come true. I just call it pure awesome-ness.

Let me break it down for you.

Y ou can control every aspect of your life experience by simply controlling the type of energy (aka: words, thoughts, attitude, mentality) you put out to the world.

You may have heard some of these familiar statements:

Like attracts like.

What you think about you bring about.

What you focus on expands.

What you put out you get back.

This is all good stuff (and true), but let me simplify it even further.

YOU ARE A HUGE, SUPER POWERFUL MAGNET.

Each moment of every day you get to decide what you want to attract into your life.

If you show up with your Ego on your sleeve you will attract others just like you. So you'll end up surrounded by Negative Nellies and Ego-driven eggheads that will pull you down.

If, however, you stand in the light and look for ways to consistently view things from a positive perspective, positive people will be drawn to you.

These positive people will (obviously) have positive effects on you. They will lift you up and present opportunities that will ultimately make up your life experience.

How you are and *how you show up* in life
will very much determine how your life
will unfold, simply based on who you
attract into your experience.

Now that's some damn good shi*f*t.

Shi*f*ting
is
not
all
about
YOU.

Globally

You can change the world.

With every shift you take, you will contribute an amazing, positive, radiant, on-fire energy that the world very much needs right now.

By shifting on the inside, you can positively affect everything and everyone on the outside.

You don't have to take my word for it. A simple 5-minute experiment will prove this.

The next time you're walking down the street, in the park, through the office or in a shopping mall, think of something that makes you happy.

Then let your facial expression reflect that feeling.

You will probably smile. Your eyes will light up, your forehead will unfurl and your walk will take a different stride.

Your shoulders will relax and your breathing will change.

N ow, make eye contact with the people in your sur-
roundings, and observe *their* reaction to *you*.

Watch what happens.

People will feed off your positive energy. Their eye contact
will be longer. They will smile back. You may even get approached more often.

Why?

Because you've given them a gift; and as a result they will *feel*
different. And you will see that difference on the outside –
through their actions.

What you won't see is the difference you are making on the
inside of each person and the collective world. By simply radiating
a mentality that encourages, elevates and energizes, you are
changing people. You are changing the world by giving people
what they very much need…

Good vibrations.

Mmmm. Delish.

Q.

If there are so many benefits to shifting, why isn't everyone doing it?

A.

For the same reason we're not all Yale graduates. Some people don't want to work that hard. Some have really thick heads that keep them from seeing the benefits.

Don't worry about them. You've got a job to do, now go do it you fabulous little shi*f*t head. I'm rooting for ya every step of the way.

You are going to be amazing.

And gorgeous too.

Shift happens

Actually, it doesn't.

F or shift to happen there are a few **prerequisites** that must be met first.

Trying to shift before doing these would be like trying to put your pants on before your underwear.

It just won't work.

You could do it, but it would be very uncomfortable.

Awkward even.

Before you shift
you have to
ADMIT,
COMMIT
and
SUBMIT.

Admit

To be a shi*f*t head you have to admit that
the way you're showing up in life
could stand some changing.

It's OK.

Admit it.

The first step in the self-development process is to become aware of the role you're playing in your own life.

By taking a good hard look, you'll identify the areas that could benefit from some tweaking.

This was pivotal for Amy.

When she started her coaching work with me, she was, well...shall I say, "unaware."

Her biggest issue at the time was that she couldn't figure out why she didn't have many friends, and why she couldn't keep the few she did have.

The truth was, Amy's sarcastic (albeit witty) ways of reacting to the world were repelling people like a bottle of OFF repels a campground mosquito. She was stinky, and no one wanted any part of her.

At first, Amy was perfectly happy to blame everyone else:

> *"They're not thick-skinned or*
> *intelligent enough to get my humor."*

She also tried to play the authenticity card:

> *"I want to stay true to myself and not*
> *bend to anyone else's expectations."*

And of course, she was fine with attributing this part of her to some external source that made it impossible to change:

> *"I get my wit and sarcasm from my*
> *father. I was born this way. There is*
> *no way to get rid of it."*

s her coach, I helped her see she had two options (you always have at least two).

OPTION #1:

Amy could continue to blame everyone and their brother for not having friends. In other words, she could take *zero* responsibility for her life being the way it was.

OR

OPTION #2:

She could take responsibility for the fact that she is playing the starring role in her reality. She could admit that how she was reacting and responding to people was the sole reason she had no friends.

Lucky for her,
she chose
Door #2

I invited her to engage in some self-observation.

I asked her to pick three people she knew who had lots of friends and to observe how they were "being". Then I asked her to observe how *she* was being and to compare notes. Obviously, the differences were dramatic.

Amy started to realize that the way she was reacting to the world, the way she was "showing up," was a direct cause of her friendless state of affairs.

The way she was "being" was not working for her, no matter how hard she tried to convince herself it was.

Through tenacity and a desire to change her life, she got to a point where she was willing to take responsibility.

She was finally
willing to

admit

she

was

the

reason

she had
no friends.

W hen she did, it was ugly and uncomfortable. It was oh so difficult to admit that she didn't have it all figured out. But once Amy admitted she was responsible for her life being the way it was, she was one step closer to fixing it.

And, guess what?

Amy has friends now. Lots of them, actually.

But if it weren't for **admitting that she needed to do something different** she could not have made some very important changes in her life to get the results she very much wanted...and deserved.

Mega, super, turbo-charged.

If you want to fix anything, you have to first recognize what is not working.

Do some self-observation.
Be a self-voyeur.
Observe your reactions and your results.

Be with them.

Criticize them and examine how they
currently define your life.
Then ask yourself if they are getting
you the results you want.
If not, admit it.

Out loud, say these words…

"I admit
that if I want to
change my Reality
I must start by
changing my Reactions."

If

R = R

(Reactions = Reality)

then

CR = CR

(Crappy Reactions = Crappy Reality)

therefore

PR = PR

(Positive Reactions = Positive Reality)

It's mathematically sound.
I rest my case.

Commit

Commit to change what
is not working.

If you want to be a shi*f*t head, a certain amount
of commitment is required — for no other reason than
it might get tough.

And when the
going gets
tough...

Right here, right now
make a commitment to yourself that
you are in this for keeps.

Here's why.

Throughout this process you will be tempted to turn back,
give up, surrender to your old ways and settle for your old reality.

But know this:

Your chances of successfully becoming
a *shift* head are **1000x** more probable
if you make a commitment.

Why do you think we sign contracts?
To get buy-in, assurance, legal recourse when
buyer's remorse sets in.

It works, right?

So, say it out loud.
Tell a friend.
Write it down.

Do something that will contractually bind you to making these necessary changes in the way you react to life.

Committing doesn't mean there is no room for failure.
If it did, our divorce rate wouldn't be at 50%.
It does, however, set you up with a more powerful mindset.

So again, be gentle with yourself.
This isn't life or death we're dealing with here...just life.

My commitment

Time... Last Saturday
Place... Portland, OR
Lesson... Blame sucks

I made a commitment to my husband to stop blaming him for everything.

Although I still catch myself doing it once in a while, since I made the promise *out loud* to stop blaming him, it makes me try harder.

Last Saturday morning while walking my dog, I saw the neighborhood cat chasing an injured baby bird. The bird could run but not fly, so it took cover under a rhododendron bush. I ran toward the cat to shoo it away, and then I checked on its prey.

The tiny bird was scared to death. I could see (and hear) its mama squawking in a nearby tree in helpless horror.

I went into superhero mode.

I hauled ass back to the house where I told my husband that I was going to get a shoe box for the injured baby bird. I was huffing and rushing because there was obviously a life on the line.

From upstairs, my husband insisted that I use rubber gloves and told me I could find them in the garage "on top of the box." I ran to the garage, and in my head I was already blaming him for breaking my flow by insisting that I use rubber gloves.

I frantically looked for "the box" on which the gloves were supposed to be located. Side note: we were in the middle of a move, so there were roughly 32 boxes in the garage.

After a whole 20 seconds of not finding them...

I went into super blame mode.

I f you could have read my mind you would have heard something like this:

"On the box? What box? Damn it! Would it be asking too much to say exactly where the gloves were? I am wasting time here. Why does he want me to wear gloves anyway? If he weren't such a germ-a-phobe, I'd already be out there rescuing that poor helpless bird. I am sure the bird is dead already, and it's all because my husband can't give clear directions. Why does he do this to me?"

...and on I went until I caught myself mid-sentence. My words echoed in my head, and I realized how absolutely ridiculous I sounded.

I giggled to myself and said, "Oh, shi*f*t!"

D on't get me wrong. It wasn't always this way.

Before working on this, the scene would have played out with me stomping in the house and telling him how frustrated he made me, and then saying something to make him feel guilty about letting that cat kill the bird.

So lame, right?

Instead, because I had made a commitment to him, when I finally found the gloves, I ran into the house and thanked my husband for being so damned thoughtful.

Then he grabbed the shoebox, I put on the gloves, and together we went out to rescue the bird.*

Make a commitment. It works.

I promise.

Yes, the bird lived to tell about it.

Submit

Submit to the process.
Surrender your Ego.
Trust your Self.

Sometimes you need to give your power away in order to get it back.

T his is one of those times.

When you submit to this shifting process, at first you may feel like you have lost control – given in, settled.

Au contraire mon frère!

That is your beloved Ego speaking.

Remember, the Ego likes pain and struggle and it's not fond of you discovering ways to take those feelings away.

Your Ego is no dummy. It knows that shifting the way you react to life will reduce struggle and relieve pain. And it just can't have that.

So it will fight. Hard.

Whenever you feel resistance to shifting, that's your Ego fighting to be heard.

Point your finger at it and say:

"Adios Amigo!
There's a new sheriff in town.
Pain and suffering
have now been outlawed."

Then get your guns out, remove the safety, aim right between the eyes and say "Oh, shift!" Then say it again. And again.

Blow holes in it until it drops to its knees.

N ow, your Ego isn't just going to take that once and say *"Sayonara!"* It will always be the other part of you. You just have to keep shooting it down. The yin and the yang must co-exist. What would a hill be without a valley? Flatlined.

And that's what *you* will have to be before you get to stop working at this. There is no arrival where you get to say, "Ok. I'm done."

Don't worry. It will get easier as you continue to practice this. But there will be times when you'll have to be on your guard with your gun out of the holster.

Sharp shootin'.

W hen I am having an *Ego-Flare-Up,* I can feel it in my core.

It's the worst when I don't like the way someone is acting. The first thing my Ego wants to do is start bitching about it. You know how it goes...

> *"She must think the world revolves around her. Doesn't she know it's rude to show up ten minutes late to everything?"*
>
> OR
>
> *"God, he's such an ignorant jerk. How could he say that in front of everyone?"*

My Ego rips into them and it's all in the name of pain. It loves to roll around in the misery caused by other people.

My Self, on the other hand, just wants to accept those people for how they really are. Celebrate them and their unique individuality. Allowing their positive attributes to have positive effects on me and my experience.

And yes, it's tough.

I have to consistently work at shooting my Ego down to let my Self shine its light. And when I do, it is so damn bright I need shades.

Try it. You'll love it.

Submitting to the process means

trusting that your Self will lead you to joy.

Every effort you put forth.
    Every time you shoot down the Ego
        and let the Self sing its song
            you are creating a momentum
                that will push you forward.

            YES!
            Forward.
                That's where you're heading.

                To a place where flowers are
                always in bloom and
                the air smells sweet.

A place where you can experience life
as it's meant to be lived –
in a state of happiness,
positivity and f 'in peace.

                And arriving there is so possible
                once you know how to apply...

The *f*'in shift

This is how you do it.

T hink for a moment about the past five days.

How many crappy situations did you have to deal with? Big or small.

Consider them all.

Now think about your spouse, partner, best friend, neighbor, children, siblings, your hair stylist and your lawn guy.

How many did they face?

Think for a moment about the last hour.

At this very moment.
What are you fretting about right now?

The possibilities are endless. There is no shortage of things for us to feel crappy about. Actually, there are about as many crappy situations as there are bagels in New York.

I mean crunch the freaking numbers…

Depending on what your mother was like or how much you were teased in grade school, you arrive to adulthood with your own set of issues.

X

Multiply that by the amount of different energy sucking people and situations your life presents you with daily.

Combine that with whether or not you take happy pills, are neurotic, eat meat, exercise or have kids.

=

And you've got an UNLIMITED amount of scenarios and situations that a standard boilerplate approach to shifting just won't cover.

That said, you might be surprised to learn that Billy Bob from Iowa who wakes up to a popped gasket on his John Deere could shift his situation the same way Susie in Manhattan, who just locked herself out of her apartment would.

Truth is, I would tell Billy Bob and Susie how to shift the same way I would tell you…

Go *f* yourself

To f yourself you

use the f in shift to:

reframe a crappy situation

so you can
take control of your reactions

and therefore
take control of your life.

Check it out…

The *f* in shift represents

*f*LIP, *f*IND or *f*REAK

*f*LIP

means to turn the situation on its head so you can look at it from a completely different angle. These are catch-alls and work for your everyday standard crappy situations. It requires some thought, but less than the others.

*f*IND

means to seek something that you are not readily seeing. When you find it, your perspective will change. A bit more effort and thought needed here, but so worth it.

*f*REAK

means to do something different, odd or irregular. You know, like a freak. Do not underestimate the power of these. They work wonders when you are in a situation that elevates your emotions and makes you feel like you're going to bust a vein. Life savers for sure…and fun too.

These are your f'in strategies.

These strategies will help you improve your
situation by shifting your perspective.

They help you react
in a way that serves you.

They help you avoid unnecessary pain,
physical and mental stress, arguments and broken hearts.

They help bring
peace, harmony and joy to your life.

They help you
take your power back.

They help you control
the outcome of your life.

It's like a menu of
f'in solutions.

✺

Here's what you do when you come
face-to-face with a crappy situation.

1

Observe your knee-JERK reaction.
That's right. Just observe it. Notice how your
Ego wants you to react. Notice how you feel.
Then **resist** going there.
You've got better plans for your life.

2

Say "Oh, shi*f*t!" Really, say it. This won't work if you
don't say it. Hence the title of this book.

3

Choose ONE *f* 'in strategy from the chart on page 173 to
reframe your crappy situation. Depending on
your mood, the scene, or how much thinking you
want to do, choose the one that feels best. For
example, choose to *flip your focus* or *find the root*.
One is all you need.

4

Ask   yourself the corresponding question from the chart. Start with the one provided or get crazy and think of your own. Either way, it's gotta be a good question. Powerful. Thought-provoking. Definitely shift-worthy.

Note: Crafting good questions takes some practice. Spend time and have patience.

5

Answer   the question.
Do not take this one lightly. This is where the shift happens. Your Ego will fight this. Find your Self and let it sing.

6

Feel the shift.   Love the **result.**

Here are the goods...

*f***LIP**	*f***LIP** the focus	What is abundant here?
	*f***LIP** your belief/opinion	What belief or opinion would serve me better?
	*f***LIP** your feelings	How do I deserve to feel?
	*f***LIP** your expectations	What good can come from this?
*f***IND**	*f***IND** the message	How does this fit into the bigger picture?
	*f***IND** a reason	Why did this *need* to happen?
	*f***IND** the benefit	How could this actually benefit me?
	*f***IND** something nice to say	Whom or what can I compliment or say something nice to?
	*f***IND** something to be grateful for	What about this situation can I be grateful for?
	*f***IND** the root	What is actually upsetting me?
	*f***IND** the truth	What information am I lacking?
	*f***IND** the opportunity	What can I turn this into?
*f***REAK**	Imitate Buddha, Jesus or any other great one.	What would He/She do?
	Laugh at the irony of the situation.	What is ironically funny here?
	Take deep abdominal breaths and count to 12.	What will I let go of?
	Think of someone worse off than you.	Who would love to switch places with me?
	Say, "Oh well, big deal, so what, who cares." in order, three times fast.	How much of my energy and emotion does this situation really deserve?

(Note: this is NOT an exhaustive list of ways to f yourself, but it will get you started.)

Baby shi*f*t first

Start small with this.
Baby steps.
At first, you'll be *f* 'ing yourself
when you are faced with things like:

crappy people, lame-o meetings, flat tires, bad hair, arriving late, fender benders, lost luggage, bad service and traffic jams.

Doing so will make a huge difference in your life.
All these baby shi*f*ts will collectively change your life so much
it will shock the shi*f*t out of you.

W hen you nail this at its foundational level, you will be much more equipped to apply it to virtually anything life throws you.

Take your time with this.

I am not suggesting that you apply this concept to some big tragic issue in your life right out of the gate.

This shi*f*ting process is best done at a micro level *first* then *later* you can apply it at the macro level for things like: divorce, death, illness, bankruptcy, getting fired/laid off and other life-changing events.

It's kind of like needing your first grade alphabet lesson before you can conquer the periodic table.

So go easy on yourself. This is a process. You have to crawl before you walk.

Oh, and it's not a race. It's your life.

Examples anyone?

CRAPPY SITUATION: Your husband forgot to pick up your prescription at the pharmacy like you asked him to do.

OBSERVE AND RESIST the knee-JERK reaction to get pissed off and tell him how you can't depend on him for anything.

SAY: "Oh, shi*f*t!"

CHOOSE: *f*LIP your focus.

ASK: "What is abundant here?"

ANSWER: My husband actually does a lot of things for me. Like that time he went to Wal-Mart to buy me tampons...?

RESULT: You tell him it's no big deal and thank him for trying. Bonus: You've avoided both a nasty discussion that will lead nowhere and your blood pressure going through the roof.

Good lovin'.

CRAPPY SITUATION: Some unrealistically tight deadlines are handed down to you at work.

OBSERVE AND RESIST the knee-JERK reaction
to complain, moan and gossip.

SAY: "Oh, shi*f*t!"

CHOOSE: *f*IND the opportunity.

ASK: "What can I turn this into?"

ANSWER: A chance to highlight my ability to perform well under pressure.

RESULT: You calmly and coolly respond with an "I'll handle that!" and your boss sees you as a shining star.

Mega-cool.

CRAPPY SITUATION: Your friend Anne cancels lunch plans with you for the umpteenth time.

OBSERVE AND RESIST the knee-JERK reaction to take it personally and rip her a new one.

SAY: "Oh, shi*f*t!"

CHOOSE: *f*IND the truth.

ASK: What information am I lacking?

ANSWER: When you ask Anne why she keeps breaking plans with you, she confides in you that her husband doesn't want her to spend any more money on lunches out, and she was embarrassed to tell you.

RESULT: A clear reminder that it is not always about you. And you avoid hitting Anne while she is down. Whew!

This, my friends, is the power behind the *f* 'in shi*f*t.

CRAPPY SITUATION: Your company plans yet another boring team building retreat.

OBSERVE AND RESIST the knee-JERK reaction
to dread the day because you believe it is a 'big waste of time.'

SAY: "Oh, shi*f*t!"

CHOOSE: *f*REAK and think of someone worse off than you.

ASK: "Who would love to switch places with me?"

ANSWER: My cousin Jason who doesn't even have a job, let alone a company that invests in its people like mine does.

RESULT: You show up at the retreat feeling super fortunate. You have fun and contribute to the team spirit!

Are you getting
the hang of this?

Thank you?

Year... 2008
Place... Portland, OR
Lesson... Gratitude rocks

I was stopped for speeding (80 in a 55) and I was so sosoosoooo angry at myself. I was so mad, it was difficult for me to resist my knee-JERK reaction in the moment (banging my fists on the steering wheel and yelling obscenities).

I *hate* spending money on traffic tickets. (Never mind that I'm breaking the law.)

As I watched the officer approach my car from my rearview mirror, I started to feel resentment toward him.

Enter my Ego:

"What a crappy job to have. Doesn't he feel bad pulling people over all day? How does he sleep at night knowing he has ruined so many people's days?"

I was clearly pissed off – at him.

Luckily though, I was smart enough to know that an attitude like that wouldn't get me far with the law (or in life).

So, in true shi*f*t head form, I tried hard to *observe* and *resist*.

Then, of course, I said, "Oh, shi*f*t!"

I t was right around Thanksgiving so I had the whole attitude of gratitude going on and before I knew it, I was rolling down the window and listening to myself say the words:

"Thank you, officer."

Yep, I thanked the guy for pulling me over. And yes, he was as shocked as I was. But as I listened to myself talk, it made sense.

I was driving too fast, which was dangerous not only to myself but to others. It was this guy's job to keep the road safe, and I was *grateful* for that.

It was almost like an out-of-body experience. I could hear the words, but I couldn't believe I was saying them.

He went back to his car with my license and registration, and I actually felt okay. By taking that "attitude of gratitude" and saying "thank you" out loud to him, I actually calmed myself down.

W hile the cop was in his patrol car writing up what I figured would be about a $250 citation, I was texting my husband to tell him what I did. I was giggling as I recounted it all. How freaking stupid and yet genius I was all in a span of five minutes.

Not a minute later the cop was at my window...

...handing me a warning.

Unbelievable, I know.

I swear this really happened.

This shift works.

It's so awesome and so much fun once you get the hang of it.

Something this fun
should be illegal.

OK, LET'S REVIEW.
This is easy. You've got this.

When you come face-to-face with a crappy situation:

ONE
Observe and resist your knee-JERK reaction.

TWO
Say "Oh, shi*f*t!"

THREE
Choose an appropriate *f* 'in strategy
to reframe your crappy situation.

FOUR
Ask yourself an *f* 'in question.

FIVE
Answer it.

SIX
Feel the shi*f*t.

Ahhhhh!

Let's shoot the shift

Put holes in it, if you dare.

Anyone can be a shi*f*t head.

This is not rocket science.

That's why when I tell potential shi*f*t heads about this simple method, they resist and try to shoot holes in the theory to challenge its simplicity.

And that's good.
I love a challenge.

The conversation normally goes something like this:

PSH *(Potential Shift Head):* Are you serious? You expect me to believe that by saying a few words out loud and thinking something different I am going to change my life?

JP: I don't expect you to believe anything that doesn't feel right to you. I *am* offering up a different way to go about your life. The cool thing is it's your choice.

PSH: *(in slightly sarcastic tone)* Okay. I'll bite.

JP: Are you sure? Because this won't work if you really aren't into it or don't believe it. I mean, it would be like an atheist showing up at church on Sunday. And I don't need to tell you how ridiculous that would be. Again, this is your choice and you get to believe what you want.

PSH: I get it. Let's get to the problem. There is this really pathetic guy at work that annoys the hell outta me. He thinks he's king and deserves all the credit. I do most of the work and he gets all the praise. It drives me nuts, and frankly I am at a point where I can't take much more.

JP: How does this guy make you feel?

PSH: What do you think? Pissed off as hell!

JP: So is it safe to assume you want something different from that part of your life experience?

PSH: Yes. I'll admit that.

JP: And do you commit to doing something different than what you have been doing?

PSH: Now, *this* sounds like church.

JP: Well it *is* a philosophy with a pretty strong following...

PSH: Yes, I commit to doing things differently.

JP: And are you willing to submit yourself to the process and try on new ways of thinking and doing so you can get different results?

PSH: Sure.

JP: Now I've got to give you some tough love. You have to face the fact that the people of the world are not here to serve *you*. And you can't make them. You have no control over what others do and say. None.

PSH: Wait a minute. I didn't say I wanted people to serve me. I just want them to be different so they're not so annoying.

JP: You want other people to be different? How long have you been trying to hike that hill? People are who they are. They show up in your life exactly the way they're supposed to. You can't control anything except the way you react to them. They are annoying because you have defined them that way. If you say they are annoying and pathetic, they will be annoying and pathetic. You get to determine your reality. And until you face that truth you can do nothing to change it.

PSH: In light of the fact that I committed to doing something different, I'll go with it.

JP: Right on. So, here is where you get to shi*f*t the situation and get your power back. Remember, whenever you let yourself react negatively to the way someone is being, you have given up your power to them. Relinquished it. Handed it over. You are letting them control you. So by choosing to see the situation differently, you never give it up, you are always in control. And you *so* deserve that.

PSH: I'm listening.

JP: First, I invite you to say the two magic words.

PSH: Oh, shi*f*t!

JP: Nice. You are halfway to shi*f*ting the situation and getting your power back. Funny what one little "f" can do, huh?

PSH: Mmm. We'll see.

JP: Now go *f* yourself.

PSH: What???

JP: Refer back to your list of crafty moves that will help you react differently. Remember, *f*LIP, *f*IND and *f*REAK.

PSH: OK, *f*LIP.

JP: Now choose what you want to *f*LIP. Your focus? Your expectations? Your feelings? Your opinion? What?

PSH: Well, I can't change my opinion about him. He is an idiot and that's that.

JP: Apparently we should start there.

PSH: How do you expect me to change my opinion about a guy I know is 110% pure pathetic-ness?

JP: Well, you could start with telling your Ego to pipe down. You can recognize that he's not exactly the kind of person you would hang out with, but thinking of him as pathetic is, as you said, "driving you nuts". It doesn't seem like this belief is serving you at all. Now, choose different words to describe him. What is the opposite of idiotic and pathetic?

PSH: I don't know. Smart and competent?

JP: Good. What's this guy's name?

PSH: Jack.

JP: You are going to *f*LIP your belief about Jack by changing the words you use to describe him.

PSH: What? Like saying that Jack is smart and competent? Yeah right! No way. He's so not smart *or* competent.

JP: Alright, if you say so.

PSH: This is really stretching it now. If you knew this guy you would agree with me. Jack is like the biggest loser I know.

JP: Actually, I wouldn't agree with you, because in doing so I would be setting myself up for disappointment, frustration, anger and pain every time I saw Jack. And I am just not that into self-sabotage and emotional mutilation. But it sounds like you are. So are you willing to submit to this process and try something new, or not?

PSH: Geez. Tough crowd. Fine…Jack is smart and competent.

JP: Now say it like you mean it.

PSH: Jack is smart and competent!

JP: Good, now let's add a little ƒREAK. Say it again but with a big smile on your face.

PSH: This is ridiculous.

JP: Look, you have two choices in life. You get to choose **happy** or **crappy**. I am fine if you choose crappy, but don't come complaining to me about it. I know better. I know that you can live happily by simply changing your perspective and getting control of your thoughts and actions. That way you can get different results - and be happy! Let me help you with this one. Tell me something that Jack *is* actually good at.

PSH: Umm…He is a decent public speaker.

JP: Good. What else?

PSH: Well, I hate to admit it but he closes like 90 percent of his sales calls. It's actually the highest in the group.

JP: Cool. What else.

PSH: Isn't that enough?

JP: What else is Jack good at?

PSH: He dresses really well, I guess.

JP: Good. Now tell me about Jack and do it with a smile.

PSH: Jack is a guy I work with who is a decent public speaker, a good salesman and a good dresser.

JP: How does that feel?

PSH: Unnatural. Uncomfortable. Ridiculous.

JP: Perfect! When anything feels uncomfortable that means you are stretching and growing.

JP: Say it again.

PSH: Jack is a guy I work with who is a decent public speaker, a good salesman and a good dresser!

JP: More creative with your language. Add some *f*REAK!

PSH: Jack is this cool dude I work with who rocks on the platform, is a killer salesman and a sharp dresser!

JP: That was ridiculously freaky. But you obviously get the point. Now how do you feel when you think about Jack?

PSH: Better actually. At least for now. Although when I see him again I'm sure all those original feelings will come back.

JP: What can you do to stay in this mindset when you see him next?

PSH: I guess I could say this weird statement again to myself.

JP: Good idea. Then when you've got that down you can graduate to actually saying it out loud to someone else. Now, that's cool. And if you really want to take control of your life you can one day aspire to tell Jack directly to his face! Imagine that.

PSH: I think I'll start with me for now.

JP: That is the smartest thing I've heard you say all day.

So, how will this PSH change his life once he gets the hang of this?

Great question.

When he starts to control the way he reacts to things that happen in his daily life by f'in himself with a fLIP, fIND or fREAK, he'll start to recognize the benefits it brings him and he'll be hooked.

Once he's hooked he'll want to do more and more of it. He'll be looking for ways to shi$f$t every situation.

It will be like a really fun game that he always wins. This is the moment he'll go from being a Potential Shi$f$t Head to being a Bona Fide Shi$f$t Head.

It is the insistent and consistent effort
that transforms him from
a wanna-be to the real deal.

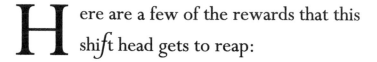

H ere are a few of the rewards that this shift head gets to reap:

✓ He will feel happier and more positive, which will be so attractive to others they will be drawn to him like mosquitoes to a bug light.

✓ His relationships will be richer.

✓ He will be more productive and intentional, and less resentful and hateful.

✓ He will be healthier as he maintains his heart rate and blood pressure at a nice, steady rate.

✓ He will be in control of his life.

The benefits are endless.
It's a snowball effect
and it all starts with saying

the words…Oh, shift!

When the shift hits the fan

Inevitable roadblocks and resistance.

I magine for a moment that you are Pac Man.

Follow me here.

You're chugging along, at a nice speed, enjoying the ridiculous electronic music in the background with a big cheesy grin on your big yellow head.

Life is good.

And then you see them. In the distance, these freaking ghost monsters all start coming toward you at once. You take a left and they go left. You head toward the corner and they follow.

They are on you like white on rice, and their mission is to gobble you up. They don't like the beat to which you are dancing. You are ruining everything for them and they want you stopped — dead. They were just fine until your smiley ass came around and caused them to stir.

Oh, and they are mad, at least they look mad. I mean what do they have to be happy about? They were pretty much pro-grammed to be pissed off by default and to gobble up anyone that looks or acts different than them.

And you do.

Look at you. Dancing around, eating up all the frickin' dots and fruit, and achieving high scores like your shift doesn't stink.

Look at *them*. They don't even have a mouth to smile with, just a shifty set of eyes, peeking out from behind their colorful (protective) moo moo.

H ere comes the ugly truth...

Brace yourself.

These ghost monsters are your friends and family that CAN'T HANDLE YOUR SHI*f*T!

Not ALL your friends and family. Just the ones that CAN'T HANDLE YOUR SHI*f*T!

They love you. They really do, and they want the best for you. The problem is that some of them think the "best" is the route *they're* taking. So when you deviate from what everyone else is doing, they want to bring you back with the pack. Where it's "normal".

But remember...

Normal ≠ Good

Now, it's not like these people are consciously setting out to envenom you with their negative thinking and grim outlook on life. They don't mean to do harm. This is just how they are and, up until now, so were you.

Then you decided to shi*f*t.

f'in yourself all over the place. Holding yourself responsible for the way you react to life. You are *f*lipping, *f*inding, *f*reaking and all is going well.

And one day (more or less)…

…you show up like the shi*f*t head you are

and they notice that you…

refuse to join in on their gossip rants,

react with grace instead of anger to life's less fortunate happenstance,

stop complaining about the trivial,

insist on finding the silver lining,

compliment instead of criticize,

laugh instead of cry…

And they respond with…

"What the hell is going on?"

"What happened to you?"

"I'm not sure I like this."

W hy would they? Most of them haven't searched deep within themselves for truth, or worked hard at changing their lives by changing the way they react.

They may not know you are on this path, wanting and working for change.

They *do* know *you*. Or at least they *did* know you the way you used to be, and they liked you that way.

They may have even liked you *because* you were that way *(gossipy, angry, egocentric, complaining, judgmental, negative, mean, high-strung — fill in the blank with your own special words.)*

Now what are they supposed to do …with you?

This is when the shift hits the fan.

When some of your friends and family see you in full shift-head form they may start to feel a disconnect.

But not all of them…

You'll know the ones that feel disconnected by the confused and slightly disappointed look on their face when you start to react differently to life.

Some people will not be able to handle your shift, and at that point you have a choice. You can either sink under their pressure and go back to your old reality, OR you can stand strong and stay shifted.

Ask yourself:
> *Who do you want to make happy?*
> *Who deserves to hold your power?*
> *Who is meant to control your life?*
> *Who do you have to answer to?*

Them or you?

The choice is yours and it will test your resolve.

It's a good thing
you are so powerful
and mighty.

Alarmed

Year... 1991
Place... New Jersey
Lesson... Tell'em

W hen I was on a visit home from college, my mother and I were leaving to go shopping. I had forgotten about the sensitivity of our home security system and how it all worked. In my careless forgetfulness I accidentally set off the alarm. Not your ordinary alarm, but one that calls in the fire trucks and police cars simultaneously, which in our small town was a big deal.

My mother was livid, but not because I set off the alarm; after all accidents happen. She was pissed because I failed to choose the

OH-MY-GOD-THE-SKY-IS-FALLING

reaction that I had chosen in the past, one that I clearly learned from her. When my reaction was more like OH-WELL-BIG-DEAL, one that I had clearly learned at college, she laid into me.

In all fairness she was justified, kind of.

I mean, that's how I had reacted in the past, and now that I wasn't reacting in the same way, she was confused...and pissed.

And I was bummed. Really bummed.

What I learned that day — and have obviously never forgotten — is that if you're going to shift, you have to realize that it will impact others around you in ways that may not be agreeable.

It's at that moment you have a decision to make.

That day I considered putting on my drama hat to appease my mother — to give her what she very much needed from me. I love her dearly and I wanted to please her, but I couldn't.

It was no longer in me.

I wasn't who I had been.

I had shifted.

So instead I cried...like a babe. I cried because I could feel the tension, resistance and pure disappointment in my mother for me not "being" the way she knew me to be. The way I used to be. Oh, and it sucked.

I am, however, very glad that I didn't give in and show up as the drama queen I left home as. It was painful, but I stuck with it.

In hindsight, I probably should have given my mother the heads-up she deserved and told her that it's not that I didn't care; I just didn't want to make mountains out of mole hills anymore.

This was my shift and I really wanted to own it.

Instead I assumed she would understand me and all the changes I had made while I was away.

Don't do that.

Let people know you are on this path so it doesn't hit them upside the head.

It's a nice gesture.

Scared shiftless

Literally.

Although I have done many things and had many successes, I am haunted by the belief (from childhood) that I can't do this or that because I'm not as smart as others. Change is difficult, and I seem to be afraid sometimes to go ahead and do something different in case it won't be any better than what I am doing now. Doubt and fear are the biggest culprits in holding me back from living my bliss.

Sherry C., 51

YOU

are your own worst enemy when it comes to change. Actually, it's not all of you, it's your Ego. And it's fugly.

It rules your Self through fear.

You know this.

Fear keeps us from success, happiness, love and achievement - all the things we most want in life.

And fear can definitely keep us from shifting.

The top 5 fears

that keep people from shifting.

Are you ready for this?

Fear #1

I won't be entertaining, witty or funny anymore.
I will be boring.

*My wine club of six years stopped calling me when
I told them I didn't want to people bash anymore.
They said that was one of the funnest things we did
together. I was literally outcast from the group
because, as one gal put it, I was 'a buzz killer.'*

Sandy K., 33

How sad. Fun doesn't have to come at the expense of
others. Funny is also possible without being negative. If
your Ego has been doing stand-up for most of your life, it's not
funny. It's rude. Howard Stern does that, and you see how far
that got him. *Hmm.* Bad example.

There's only room for one at the top of that trash heap, and
Stern has claimed it. Let him have it.

There are tons of people who are entertaining, witty and funny
without being negativity mongers and making others look bad.
Ellen DeGeneres comes to mind. Wouldn't you love to be in
her wine club?

Fear #2

I will lose some of my friends.

Yes you will. And thank goodness for that. Were they really friends to begin with? The people who are attracted to you for your Ego-driven ways are the same ones that will fall off when you shift.

Take stock. Who in your life needs to be flushed out?

In my research for this book, one PSH told me:

It seems that as I became more positive, certain people drifted out of my life. It wasn't actually anything I did, but I found we just didn't have as much in common. I had been friends with Kathy for almost 20 years. We always loved to share our problems. When I began to love my life and not want to spend time talking about the bad stuff, it just wasn't the same. Once she was no longer in my life, it opened me up to meeting other people who I totally adore. I am thrilled with these new friends. They are just like me!

Katherine M., 61

Be wary of friends who think complaining and whining is FUN. What does that say about them? Better yet, what does that say about you having them as your friends?

Double ouch.

Fear #3

People will think I'm a Pollyanna.

When you are lying on your deathbed,

will you be wishing

you were known

as a jerk

or a

Zen

monk?

Fear #4

I'll be a pushover and lose my edge.

T his is another good one. You may think if you squash out the Ego you will surrender the business skills, cut throat mentality or negotiating edge that you "need" to get ahead.

Read this great Aesop fable, and then decide if brutal force is the only way to get what you want.

THE WIND AND THE SUN

The Wind and the Sun were disputing which was stronger. Suddenly they saw a traveler coming down the road, and the Sun said, "I see a way to decide our dispute. Whichever of us can cause that traveler to take off his cloak shall be regarded as the stronger. You begin." So the Sun retired behind a cloud, and the Wind began to blow as hard as it could upon the traveler. But the harder he blew the more closely the traveler wrapped his cloak around him, until at last the Wind had to give up in despair. Then the Sun came out and shone in all his glory upon the traveler, who soon found it too hot to walk with his cloak on.

"KINDNESS EFFECTS MORE THAN SEVERITY."

Fear #5

I will fail at this.

F ail? Are you kidding me? Of course you'll fail.

Mark Twain wrote, *"Quitting smoking is easy. I've done it a thousand times."* Remember, shifting takes an insistent and consistent effort. Don't worry, or even expect to arrive all at once. Just keep your head down, stay focused and know that each situation presents another opportunity to succeed.

Stay in the moment and set your intention on making this one change in your life.

The only way you can really fail is if you *fail to try* – again and again.

Being a shi*f*t head means being a fighter, a worker bee, a disciple of your Self – a tenacious human that is conscious about how you view your world and is consistent in shifting the views that don't serve you.

And remember, you can't go on autopilot here. You never get to quit. It's kinda like mothering *(or so I hear).*

Go mama. Go.

Get your shift together

Just the FAQ's.

How can I shi*f*t
when all the news
is so negative?

Turn off the *f*reakin' news.

L ike food for your body, the news feeds your brain. Watching the news is equivalent to eating a Big Mac. It does nothing but fill you up with crap.

It might feel good going down but the consequences are brutal. Just don't do it. Cut yourself off from the news. Tell yourself it's cancerous... 'cause it's that deadly.

Now, I am not suggesting you cut yourself off completely and become an apathetic citizen.

You know the crap news I am referring to.

I guarantee you that hearing about who got hit by a car, murdered, raped or shot does not make you an "informed citizen" or help you in any way.

Turn. It. Off.

You'll be so glad you did.

How can I shift when the people I am around are so negative?

What if I live with a sh*t head and I want to be a shift head?

W ho you live with does not determine how you live. Again. *Who* you live with does not determine *how* you live.

As long as you blame others for your misfortune, lack of will or poor choices, you will be giving your power away to them.

You might as well wrap it up, tie a bow around it and hand it over to them. If you are doing this now, stop it. It's a nasty habit that's bad for your health.

If you are surrounded by people who live in a negative space, let them own it as *theirs* not *yours*. Allow them to be where they are and don't agree to join them.

Honoring people where they are is the best gift you can give them — just insist on receiving the same respect from them.

Let the sh*t heads in your life know that you are no longer willing to play in their sandbox. They can be there till they rot if they want to, but they can't drag you back in it, no matter how lonely they get in there. It's your responsibility to tell them this. You can't assume they will get it without being told.

> Set your boundaries
> and let them know about it...

And another thing.

Being a shift head is the greatest way to clean house and get rid of the bad apples that bring you down.

Those toxic, stinky types that cause you more grief than you deserve...

You know who I am talking about.

Let them go.

You make this sound so easy...

Even if they annoy
the crap out of me,
it's hard to tell people
in my life that I don't
want to, as you say,
"play in their sandbox."

D ifficult task? You bet. I'm not suggesting it's easy.
If it were you would have done it by now. And so
would everyone else.

Need some convincing? Chew on this:

- Discomfort is a necessary evil and a sure sign that you are on a path toward change.

- Do what you've always done and you'll always get what you've always gotten.

- Letting people know that you have taken back control of your life is a ballsy thing to do. Letting them go is even ballsier. But you've got a pair – so use 'em.

- You deserve to be surrounded by people who feed your soul, not suck it dry.

- You always have a choice. Always.

I'm not saying you have to
do this. I'm just thinking
you might want to.☺

As a shi*f*t head, I know so many people that I would love to see shi*f*t.

How can I help others get this?

Here's what you do…

Give a shi*f*t. But just one.

As a shift head your radar is always on. You can't help it. You will start to pick up on others' negative reactions and self-defeating behavior. It will be blaring, actually.

As a result, you will want to show others the light, and you should. **But just once.**

Be willing to show people how they could view their crappy situation from a different perspective, or how they might react in a different way to get a different result.

Get them to *f*LIP, *f*IND and *f*REAK by asking them powerful questions. Giving people the chance to change their lives is a charitable act that everyone deserves to receive.

Don't 'ya think?

N ow, here's the important part…

When you begin to show them the power of shi*f*ting, observe their response to your generous gift. If they are receptive and seem to really tune in to what you're sharing, they are probably open to more. Cool.

If not, back off.

You can't force people to jump on your gravy train. If they're not ready, you can't *make* them shi*f*t.

What am I supposed to do with the people who do not want to shi*f*t?

N othing. Simply continue to walk and talk like your shift doesn't stink. Just show up in the best way that makes you happy, knowing that's all you can do. Stand strong in the belief that this is the right path for you; and if your friends or loved ones want to join you, they will. It's that simple.

Trust me, you don't want to be like one of those hyped-up vegans or religious converts who are so adamant about getting you to drink the Kool-Aid. It's such a huge turn-off.

Those people make me want to eat a steak and join a cult.

But there are others who don't try to suck you in, they just live and let live. You know the type. They simply do their thing and could care less if you notice it or not. If you notice, and it's attractive to you, perhaps you'll follow suit. If you don't notice, then it's not meant to be on your radar at that time.

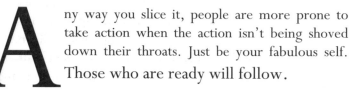

A ny way you slice it, people are more prone to take action when the action isn't being shoved down their throats. Just be your fabulous self. Those who are ready will follow.

That's the way it will be when you show up like a shift head. Those who like what they see will be open to receiving your help. Those who aren't will resist following your lead. And that's perfectly fine.

Show them the way and let them decide. The good news is that *shift headitis* is contagious. People will start to see your life changing virtually overnight, and they'll be wondering who slipped a mickey in your drink.

When they do, just pass 'em a copy of this book.

I'll have them at hello.

A tribute to shift heads everywhere:

You entered into the shift like a leaf floating down a river.
You didn't fight it. You flowed with it.
You trusted the process and didn't cling to the "safe" route.
You willingly stepped out of your comfort zone, onto the ledge.
In part because you were tired of living in a way that didn't
support you in getting what you want.
It exhausted you to keep thinking and acting in a self-defeating way.
In other words, you gave in.
You shifted, and you won.

You are a true shift head.
My hat is off to you.

That's good shift

Real stories from real shift heads doing the do.

It was 4pm on the Saturday of Memorial Day weekend.

I was getting my tank filled at a gas station near my house. As I sat there waiting, a man with a pick-up truck and a boat pulled around to the pump next to mine. This caused his boat to block me in.

The very first sarcastic thought that went through my head was, "You are kidding me, right? I *know* you are not blocking me with that big boat, mister. How rude!" I didn't say it, but I'm sure it showed on my face.

Instead of holding onto that bad thought, I shifted my thinking... I smiled and said, "Oh, shi*f*t!" I looked over at him and his son and said, "Looks like somebody is headed to the river!" He responded with, "Yep, a bit late, but what the heck?"

I said, "Oh well, better late than not at all. Besides, it doesn't get dark 'til eight so you've got plenty of time to play!"

He laughed.

He noticed the attendant had just removed the nozzle from my gas tank and asked me, "Can you get out?"

I told him I wanted to head around his boat to go in the direction I needed to go. He pulled forward a bit and allowed me to get out without delay!

Christine Rae, 42

Good for you, Christine. That's a classic *find something nice to say* that worked like a charm.

I am learning it is better to put my focus on things that I do have power over instead of the 'what ifs' that may or may not even happen.

Kevin S., 33

Scoooooooore!

I told my husband I was planning on taking Domenic...

...our toddler, to the gym with me one Saturday. He thought it was a great idea and said he would take advantage of the 'free time' to run some errands — and then bee-lined it out the door.

Packed up and ready to go, I opened the door to the garage and guess what was gone? The SUV! Yes, the SUV with the only baby car seat we own. AGH!

Now I'll admit, my first knee-JERK reaction was to call my husband an idiot (ok, an *f*'in idiot). But then I said, "Oh, shi*ft*!" out loud.

I thought, well, it *is* a beautiful day outside and we *do* have a new Radio Flyer Wagon. So I took Domenic, the wagon and even our dog Daisy, and we headed out for a walk in the neighborhood. When we got outside, we saw our neighbor Felicia, who I hadn't seen for days. I hung out with her for a little bit and then went on our walk.

It turned out not to be such a sh*tty predicament after all. I got my exercise, connected with my neighbor, the dog got a walk, Domenic had fun and my husband didn't get such a beating!"*

Lorelei W., 40

---

* *Lorelei is from New Jersey where husband beating is socially accepted.*

Katherine M. gets her power back.

JP: Tell me about some benefits you've seen as a result of your shi*f*ting.

KM: Well, I know that my relationship with my ex-husband has improved. I used to be angry with him whenever I would hear him speak. Recently, I was at a family gathering for one of our children. He was standing there talking to me and was saying some things that I definitely didn't agree with. I told him that I didn't agree with him but I was able to do it in a non-angry way. I simply said it, and he didn't get mad.

JP: How did you get to that point?

KM: By realizing that as long as you have buttons for someone to push, you are not a free person. After I walked away from that conversation I knew I didn't have buttons he could push any longer. I felt so free.

JP: Cool shift! What are some other benefits you have seen since becoming a shift head?

KM: My health. I have had really bad allergies most of my life. I went through 11 years of allergy shots, developed Candida from too many antibiotics and cortisone and developed environmental allergies from the Candida making me allergic to perfumes, odors, and molds. At times I thought I was going to die. When I began to shift, I discovered ways to become well, including changing my eating habits to include more raw fruits and vegetables and some alternative therapies.

JP:. How are you now?

KM: Today, none of those illnesses are in my life. I feel exceptionally well. In fact, I'm convinced I feel younger than when I was in my teens and 20's.

JP: Rock on, sista!

Carol L. finds the reason.

I had made plans to go visit my sister in Phoenix.

I left the house with what I thought was enough time to make it to the airport *(I hate waiting, so I admittedly cut things close).*

I parked the car in long-term parking and waited for the shuttle. I had 35 minutes before my plane took off and the shuttle took forever to arrive. When it finally did, I was so mad at the driver I could barely speak. What's worse, it was an old guy that *drove* like an old guy, so it took us double the normal time to make it to the terminal.

I busted my way out of the shuttle and rushed to check in. I was told it was too late to check my bags, which contained liquid hair products and perfume. So if I wanted to take my bag with me, I'd have to ditch anything liquid. I was enraged. I laid into the lady and told her how absolutely ridiculous that was. *Did she know how much these products cost?*

Anyway, I ran like hell to get through security and to my departing gate. Sweating, angry and really pissed off at myself for being in this position, when I got there the airline lady told me that boarding had finished and I would not be allowed on the flight.

"What do you mean I can't get on *my* flight?"

She apologized and asked me if I would like to reserve a seat on the next flight to Phoenix that was due to leave in three hours! Oh, and it would cost me an extra $75. *Aggh!*

All I could do was berate myself for being so stupid. *I should have taken the tollway to avoid traffic. I should have woken up earlier or packed the night before. I shouldn't have ditched those products! My sister's plans to pick me up at the airport were completely messed up because I was due to arrive three hours late.* And the list went on...

JP: What did you do then?

CL: Well, I was seeing red, but I knew the truth and it was killing me. There was nothing I could do to fix this. Nothing! And I hated that because I am a control freak. So I thought for a second and tried to find the reason why this was happening to me. I knew I was in this situation because I was meant to be there. But why? I wanted to know what it was all for. I was still steaming mad at this point, but at the same time I got curious.

JP: How did that help you?

CL: To be honest, that in and of itself calmed me down, or at least distracted my thoughts.

JP: What happened next?

CL: Well, once I got my wits about me I called my sister to apologetically tell her I would be coming in late. To my surprise she was relieved to hear it. Turns out she really needed the extra time to, as she put it, "get her life together" before I arrived. I went to reserve my seat, and I took a shot with the guy at the ticket counter to see if he could make an exception or put me at the end of the list to avoid having to pay the extra money for the switch. I think he took pity on me because he just winked and told me he'd take care of it.

JP: Nice!

CL: Yeah, but it wasn't until I sat down in my assigned seat that *I realized why I had missed my first flight.* I introduced myself and started to make small talk with the man in the seat next to me. As luck would have it, he was a district manager of a pharmaceutical company that I had been trying to get hooked up with for over six months! We totally hit it off, and I shared with him the ironic course of events that led me to finally meet him. We had a good laugh and I contacted him when I got home to set an appointment for the following week!

JP: Mega cool. So what did you take away from that whole experience?

CL: Whenever stuff like this happens to me, I really need to believe that it's all happening for a reason. If I just stop and trust that it will all eventually make sense, I can maintain a bit more control.

JP: Control of what, exactly?

CL: My emotions, I guess. It is not always easy to calm myself down in the moment, but when I do, I function at a higher level. I realize now that I could have saved myself all that pain and frustration if I had just accepted the situation for what it was and shifted my perspective sooner rather than later. Live and learn!

Tom C. chooses abundance.

JP: Tom, what are some roadblocks or resistance you face in trying to react more positively?

TC: I don't always remember I have the power of choice. I feel victimized and powerless.

JP: Can you give me an example of a time you felt that recently?

TC: I found myself very much behind schedule today and not getting all the things done that I promised myself I'd do. My knee-JERK reaction was to blame myself. I called myself lazy, disorganized, unmotivated, and ineffective.

JP: What do you do to come out of that self-defeating place?

TC: I talk with my coach or recall the good advice she gave me, for example, remembering what I have in abundance, or celebrating my victories and accomplishments.

JP: *Flipping the focus* from what is lacking to what is abundant. Sweet glory!

Laura C. doesn't let people get the best of her.

JP: Laura, what one thing tends to trigger your Ego the most?

LC: It's easy to get hooked by other people's tone, attitude and behavior. Sometimes I get angry when I don't feel valued or appreciated by people. When people are rude, angry or mean, it's easy to want to pull away or emotionally disconnect from them.

JP: How do you react to people like that?

LC: I usually get defensive at first, and then realize they must be pretty bad off to be so nasty. When I was younger, I would stay angry and give people the silent treatment. All it did was hurt me because the anger, madness and frustration worked against the core of who I am – joyful, caring and happy.

JP: What are some strategies you use to shi*f*t your perspective?

LC: I think about what I *do* have control or influence over and remind myself that I can't be responsible for others and their words or behaviors. I say to myself, "Assume the best and leave the rest." And then I like to ask, "Will this really make a difference years from now?"

JP: Nice one.

Now, back to you.

You are the Shift

This is about YOU changing your life.

YOU, the shift head, coming to

terms with the fact that YOU

have complete control

of your life

starting

right

now.

And that's good.

Real good.

What will that control get you?

One thing.

The one and only thing you really want.

It's what you are here to experience.
It's what you were born into.

Your natural birthright...

JOY

Joy is yours.

All yours.
If you choose it.

Once you learn this.

The moment you embrace this single truth.

When you make this shift...

You are free.

Free from the prison of victimhood.
Free from pain and suffering.
Free from your Ego.
Free from confusion, indecision and regret.
Free from the epidemic of a scarcity mentality.
Free from self-doubt, blame and judgment.

And with that comes the freedom to be
who you are and live the life you desire.
The freedom to celebrate
your victories and failures equally.
You are free to succeed at anything.
You are free to find JOY wherever you look.
Simply because you choose to.

When you make this shift so many f 'in things
are going to change in your life you
won't even know what hit 'ya.

You will be happier.
You will feel powerful.
You will *be* powerful.
You will be a positive influence.
You'll attract more quality people, experiences and opportunities in your life.
Your health will improve.
Your relationships will improve.
You'll get a raise.
You'll get a job.
You'll like your job.
You'll find a partner.
You'll be more likeable to your current partner.
You'll bounce out of bed in the morning.
You will get what you want.
You will laugh more.
You will worry less.
You'll avoid disease.
You'll sleep better.
You'll make more money.
Your life will have more meaning.
You will like yourself.
You'll be liked by others.
You'll exercise more.
You'll lose weight. *(Individual results may vary)*

You'll drink less.
You'll glow.
You'll be more sane.
You'll cry less.
Your skin will clear up.
You'll discover new things.
You will see the light.
You'll avoid the dark.
Your kids will learn from the best.
Your parents will be proud.
You'll be better looking.
You'll smell better. (really)
You'll like, maybe love, your life.
Your reputation will improve.
You'll live a more authentic life.
You'll model the behavior you hope to see in others.
You'll make people smile.
You'll breathe easier.
You'll be more successful.
You'll be admired and envied (in a healthy way).
You'll wear less black.
Your phone will ring more.
You'll have more energy.
You'll have fewer regrets.
You will be infectious.
You will make a difference.
You will positively contribute to the good of the universe.

You deserve this.

I love you.
I know that sounds freakin' weird, but if you haven't noticed,
I don't talk smack or say shift I don't mean.

It's true.

And if I can love you,
then you can love yourself enough
to get off your derriere and change your life.
This is your life we're talking about here.
Oh, and it's not like Costco where you get to buy endless
amounts in bulk size quantities.
You just get this one little, neatly packaged,
limited-time-only life.

Stop acting like it's disposable.

There really is no more where this came from.
Therefore, you deserve to have every single day filled with
joy, peace and success.
And it's all within your control.
Do you get that?
You were born as this little super hero
with the biggest super power of them all.
The power to choose.

Wham! BadaBOOM! Ka-POW!

It's a movement

Be a part of it.

So....

You've made the shi*f*t.

You choose JOY.

Now every decision you make, every reaction you select, every perspective you adopt will come from that place and will simultaneously lead you there.

How?

Whenever you choose
to start from joy
you incvitably end up there.

Full circle, baby.

You are so cool.

And when you're that cool *(read enlightened)* you have a job to do.

Your job is to share this with others.
That's right. Don't keep it to yourself.
It's too good, and so are you.

Your light is shining so bright you couldn't hide it if you tried.

I dare you to be a star in someone's life.
Guide them.
Show them what they can be.
Tell them it's as simple as making a choice.
Tell them about the one little letter.
Let them know that life
doesn't have to be anything less than amazing.
Remind them of their natural birthright
and tell them that they too
deserve to be on this

JOY RIDE

called

LIFE.

Choosing JOY
and lighting the path
for others to do the same.

That's what shift heads do.

This isn't just about you and me. It's about us.

All of us working together to create a shift
so big that it makes a mark on the world.

*(Seriously, I'm not exaggerating
about the world part.)*

You.
Me.
Us.

Making a mark on the world.

Here are a few ways you can start to make your mark.

ONE.

Create a shift head dinner club, shift head happy hour club, shift head networking club. Have regular meetings or irregular ones. Hold each other accountable to shifting. Share successes, obstacles and strategies. Together you will shine a brighter light than you ever could alone.

TWO.

Hold a "Get Shift-Faced Party" where your friends and family come together to lift each other up and create meaningful shifts in your lives. Think of the positive effect you will have on yourself, each other, the world. Be the one to cause the domino effect.

THREE.

Send a copy of this book to *one* friend who's ready to change his/her life by changing the way they react to it. Autograph it and tell'em you're in this together.

FOUR.

Share your Shi*ft*.

Tell people about the shifts you are making in your life. Inspire them through your stories and watch what happens.

FIVE.

Get a buddy.

My friend Heather is my "What does this mean?" buddy. Whenever something crappy happens to either one of us, we vow to call the other to discuss what message or meaning the event has for us. Both of us always hang up the phone completely shi*ft*-faced.

SIX.

Get creative.

Come up with your own shi*ft*y efforts to collaborate with others and share all your great ideas at *www.ohshift.net.*

You can do this.

I believe in you.
You have all you need to take
this small step towards big change.
Just start by saying two simple words.
If you can't say it, you can't do it.
And I *know* you can say it.

You are a rock star and your potential is colossal.
Bigger than you can imagine.
Don't waste it.
Honor it.
Say it.
Be it.

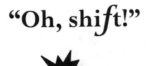

 *JENNIFER POWERS*

ACKNOWLEDGMENTS

As cliché as it may sound, this book would not be in your hands if it weren't for a few amazing individuals.

Luis...
You are my biggest fan and I love you more than words can say. Thank you for putting up with me for the nine months it took to birth this baby. Your philosophical perspectives and insights brought out my best thinking. Thank you for always, always, always supporting me and believing in me. Schmaks!

Heather Strang...
My editor. My soul sister. Thank you for honoring me *and* my voice in the editing of this book. Your belief in me and my message made this process delicious. Even more importantly, thank you for your special friendship. I am so lucky to call you my friend...and to just *call* you... any time the wind appears to be blowing in the wrong direction. I love you.

Elaine Sanchez...
Thank you for your never-ending, unconditional support, wisdom, guidance and love. Your edits and thoughtful conversations around the concepts in this book were an invaluable part of the process. You are an amazing friend. I love you.

Kent Gustavson...

My publisher. My friend. You saw in me what I couldn't see for myself. Thank you for insisting that I write this book in *my* voice. Hell, thank you for helping me *find* my voice. You are such a talented individual and I adore you and the work you do to inspire authors to share their authentic message. The publishing industry and the world are better off because of your great contributions.

Mom and Len...

You really deserve all the credit. Thank you for always wishing me nothing but happiness and encouraging me to find it. It worked. I love you.

My Coaching Clients...

You are all rock stars. Every day you teach me, inspire me and expand me. Thank you for allowing me to help you shift. It is a beautiful process to witness, and one that contributed to this book more than you know.

Thank you...

Don and Lori Waldo, (What would I do without my gorgeous, wise, witty, loving, generous sister, Lori? You are the best!) Kyle Sexton, Tim Fahndrich, Kim Rosenberg, Abigail Dougherty, Amanda Halbirt, Sally Rodgers, Della Rae, Jan Carothers, Glenda Michael, Christina Lask, Andrea Fenton, Mary Reilly, Susie Fowler, Oliver Twist Catala, Mozart Gamba. You all wow me, and I am so lucky to have you in my life. Thank you. Thank you. Thank you. Thank you. Thank you. Thank you. Thank you. Thank you. Thank you. Thank you. Thank you.

IT'S A MOVEMENT ✹

ABOUT THE AUTHOR

Jennifer Powers is a fearless, loving heart
who insists on making a difference in the
world before she checks out. She coaches,
speaks and writes from a place of honesty,
service and pure giddiness. She is a believer
in the human spirit and her mission is to
help others find their truth, whatever
that may look like. And whether she has
met you yet or not, she is your biggest fan.

Oh, and when she *does* meet you...
expect a hug.

Dog Shift.

I love dogs.
Actually, I love all animals.

That's why part of the proceeds from
this book will be donated to
The Humane Society of the United States.
www.hsus.org

Woof.

One last thing…

Thank you for being so *f* 'in beautiful.

Believing in you,
Jennifer